C000296127

NOTTINGHAM CANAL
A History and Guide

NOTTINGHAM CANAL
A History and Guide

BERNARD CHELL

TEMPUS

By the same author:
Nottingham's Lost Canal, 1995

This book is respectfully dedicated to the memory of William Jessop,
canal engineer extraordinaire.

Frontispiece: March of the swans at the junction of Robbinetts Arm and Cossall Embankment. The swans are coming off the embankment heading for the Robbinetts Arm, top right, in 1988. (Broxtowe Borough Council)

First published 2006

Tempus Publishing Limited
The Mill, Brimscombe Port,
Stroud, Gloucestershire, GL5 2QG
www.tempus-publishing.com

© Bernard Chell, 2006

The right of Bernard Chell to be identified as the Author
of this work has been asserted in accordance with the
Copyrights, Designs and Patents Act 1988.

All rights reserved. No part of this book may be reprinted
or reproduced or utilised in any form or by any electronic,
mechanical or other means, now known or hereafter invented,
including photocopying and recording, or in any information
storage or retrieval system, without the permission in writing
from the Publishers.

British Library Cataloguing in Publication Data.
A catalogue record for this book is available from the British Library.

ISBN 0 7524 3759 3

Typesetting and origination by Tempus Publishing Limited
Printed in Great Britain

CONTENTS

INTRODUCTION

My interest in the Nottingham Canal goes back over fifty years, from a time when it was still in water and fairly good condition for the whole of its 14¾-mile length to the present day. Now only the bottom 2¼ miles in Nottingham still remain in use and just a small section of approximately 200 yards at the top end of the canal at Langley Mill close to the Great Northern Basin, the junction of the Nottingham, Cromford, and Erewash canals. The remainder of the canal in between these two points is a ever-changing. In some rural areas there is still water in the canal. This water is not very deep, with less depth during the summer months. Just one exception is a small section at Awsworth still used by the Cotmanhay Angling Club.

Knowing the canal as I did when a boy, over the years I have seen great changes; the part of the canal where I spent most of my time has mostly been obliterated. This includes all the lock section from Lenton to Wollaton, a total of seventeen locks in approximately 3 miles. I can remember the canal well, as I was living within half a mile of the heavy locked section. My memories are of looking down at the water from hump-backed bridges, crossing over the locks and walking along the towpath many times.

I spent many happy hours fishing from the canal banks, moxstly in the pound between lock nos 7 and 8 and the top pound above Wollaton Colliery. It use to cost 6*d* (2½p) for a day ticket It was also a popular pastime of young children to go fishing with a net and jam jar for sticklebacks and small fish in the overflow weirs which carried the water round the locks. The canal was still in good condition then, only closed to navigation for about fourteen years.

The other activity we indulged in was swimming just above Lock No.19 at Wollaton Colliery. It was here the hot water entered the canal from the colliery. We called this 'Hotties' because the water was so nice and warm. I remember badly cutting one of my big toes on a broken bottle below Lock No.19. It is much frowned upon to go swimming in canals today, which is for the best.

It was the early 1960s when I started to take an interest in the history of our canal system, having hired boats on the Norfolk Broads for a number of years. My

Lock No.1 entrance to Nottingham Canal from the river Trent. Taken in 1921, the factories on the left have since been demolished and replaced with apartments.

wife and I, with our two young children, hired a boat from Rowton Bridge on the Shropshire Union Canal. From there, cruising the Llangollen Canal I found so much of interest I wanted to know more. It was then that I discovered the books of Charles Hadfield and L.T.C. Rolt, both authors of many canal books. These gentlemen were founding members of the Inland Waterways Association in the late 1940s. It was from reading books I came to learn of engineers like James Brindley, Thomas Telford and William Jessop, among many others. William Jessop was the engineer for the Nottingham Canal. The more I read the more I became hooked.

It was after this that I first started to trace the history of the Nottingham Canal. When I was a boy it was always known as Wollaton Canal. I found it mentioned in some books but very little had been recorded. I decided to revisit the canal I knew as a boy. I found it had changed dramatically from how I remembered it; the changes between 1953 and 1968 – a period of only fifteen years – were remarkable to say the least. Gone was the canal where I went fishing; it had changed from a complete canal through a period of some dereliction to a complete disappearance in many places. Later, from the mid-1970s, these changes increased even more with the development of new housing estates and small business parks. These covered most of the canal's route through the Wollaton and Radford area and completely engulfed the canal to such an extent only small traces of it remain

Taken fifty-five years later in 1976 from almost the same position as the picture on page 7, this photograph gives a wider view of the factory with the lock house on the left.

around here. The section of canal in Nottingham still open to navigation tells a completely different story; it has been developed greatly over the past ten to fifteen years, these changes carried out very tastefully, and retaining some of the old buildings around it creating a good mix of old and new.

The history of the Nottingham Canal is no different to that of many other canals in many ways: there were prosperous times with fair profits, a slow decline accompanied with loss of revenue, declining traffic and the onset of the railways. This was followed with selling out to the railway companies, then final closure and dereliction, returning back to the land from which it came in some areas. Remarkably, from the time the Nottingham Canal received Royal Assent on 1 January 1792 to the final committee meeting on the 4 April 1856, the period was just sixty-four years.

I

PLANS FOR A NEW CANAL

The Erewash Canal had the monopoly of waterborne traffic down the Erewash Valley, as the first and only canal in the area. It was completed in 1779. The passing of the Cromford Canal Act on 31 August 1789 would provide a connection with the Erewash Canal at Langley Milll. The Cromford Canal would serve collieries in the Amber and Derwent Valleys of Derbyshire. The Erewash Canal was already serving collieries along the Erewash Valley from the river Trent and Trent Lock to Langley Mill, and had been established for fifteen years when the Cromford Canal was completed in 1794.

The Erewash monopoly had left the collieries in Nottinghamshire without an outlet for their coal. Nottingham was still receiving coal by road, which was only carried in small amounts. Some coal did arrive in the city by water from the Erewash Canal via the river Trent, but this could not be relied on as the river was shallow in places and suffered from drought in the summer and floods during the winter. It became clear to businessmen in Nottingham that there was a danger the town could suffer a coal shortage and the Erewash Co. would have the advantage. A public meeting was called, attended by three prominent Nottingham businessmen: Thomas Oldknow, textile merchant from the town, John Morris Stocking, manufacturer, and Henry Green. The meeting was to promote a canal to run a junction with the Cromford Canal at Langley Mill to the river Trent in Nottingham below Trent Bridge.

The meeting was held at the Guildhall, Nottingham, on 26 October 1790. It was made clear by a representative of the Erewash Canal Co. who attended the meeting that Erewash would oppose the Act; they saw it as a direct threat to their own canal trade, a trade which they had dominated without opposition for some years. It was known at the time they preferred trade to come down their own canal through the Cranfleet Cut, down the river Trent and through the proposed Beeston Cut, which they supported. Although the Erewash Canal Co. explained this to the Nottingham Corporation, the Corporation decided to support the proposed Nottingham Canal Co.

The project was fully supported by the Cromford Canal Co. who saw it as a direct route into Nottingham for trade from their canal. Support also came from

William Jessop
1745–1814

Drawing of William Jessop, canal engineer. (Kevin Chell)

the Grantham Canal Co., who in turn were seeking to get their own Act through Parliament. They saw the Nottingham Canal as a link for their own trade into the city; their canal was to enter the river Trent on the opposite side almost facing the entrance to the Nottingham Canal.

The dominant cargo to be carried was coal. The boats used were the Trent type, having a beam of 14ft; these boats would carry up to 40 tons and would be purchased by the canal company at between £50 and £60 each. The charge for one man, a boy and a horse for a day's work would be 6s 9d (33½p). The cost of transporting 120 tons of coal down from Wollaton to Nottingham was £3, navigating the boat for three days £1 03d (£1 1½p), loading and unloading at wharves 4½d (2p) per ton, 120 tons £2 50d (£2 25p). Storage at the wharf 1d per ton, 120 tons 10/-d (50p). Carriage from wharf to customer's door 1/-d (5p) per ton 120 tons £6. The grand total was £12 5s 3d (£12 26½p), which was just a little over 2s 1½d (11p) per ton. This estimate appears most likely to have been for coal carried from Lord Middleton's mines close to the canal at Wollaton.

William Jessop, the prominent canal engineer of the time, was called in to carry out the survey. It was known he had done the survey for the Cromford Canal. Jessop produced his estimate in September 1791; the estimate was accepted at a public meeting on 25 October. There had been difficulties in obtaining a route that was satisfactory to all the landowners. Lord Middleton, influential in Wollaton, had proposed a route with a tunnel avoiding his land. Jessop had the last say with his route, although some modifications were made in the Wollaton area. William Jessop was possibly our greatest civil engineer, born in Devon in 1745. At the time, his father was in charge of maintaining Eddystone Lighthouse, William Jessop became apprentice to John Smeaton, an engineer at the peak of his profession, after Smeaton was called in to do work on Eddystone Lighthouse. After serving some years as apprentice until 1767, he became Smeaton's assistant until 1772, after which he became an engineer in his own right. He worked on many canals in the Midlands, Wales, Scotland and Ireland. He also worked on rivers, being responsible for the canalisation of both the Trent and Soar, and the building of West India Docks in London. He seems to be mostly remembered for his partnership with Benjamin Outram in the Butterley Co., producing ornamental cast-iron bridges used during the canal era. The company is still in existence today, having recently produced the steel fabrication work for the Falkirk Wheel built to lower boats from the Union Canal to the Forth and Clyde Canal in Scotland, which opened in 2002 at a cost of £84.5 million.

The estimate submitted by William Jessop was:

Cost of Works for Nottingham Canal

Common Cuttings	£5,015
5 Deep Cuttings	£5,294
4 Embankments	£1,745
20 Locks	£9,200
12 Road Bridges	£1,020
42 Occupation Bridges	£2,940
Culverts and Drainage	£248
Fencing, gravelling towpath	£1,600
Purchase of land	£6,270
Temporary drainage	£0,500
Caliginous of above	£3,383
Reservoirs	£7,000
Greasley Bank	£200
Cossall Bank	£260
Sneinton Branch	£510
Beeston Meadow Branch	£4,735
Total	£49,920

The Beeston Meadow Branch included in William Jessop's estimate was dropped by the Nottingham Co. due to opposition from the Trent Navigation Co.; they were not prepared to forward money towards construction, but insisted that all tolls received from traffic passing through this branch be paid to them.

There were great celebrations in Nottingham when the Act for the canal received Royal Assent. The church bells were set ringing for the occasion.

With the difficulties over the route agreed to the satisfactory of the landowners, the Act called for the canal to run from a junction with the Cromford Canal to a junction with the river Trent below Trent Bridge, passing through the parish of Eastwood on the lands of John Plumtree, Elizabeth and Mary Newall, John Hanford, John Day and Gervous Bourne. From there it would continue to the parish of Greasley and the lands of the Earl of Stamford and Lord Viscount Melbourne, then onto the lands of Lord Middleton and the Earl of Stamford, again in the parish of Nuthall. It would then pass through Cossall Common to the lands of Tristram Exley, Isaac Pickthall and Edward Willoughby in the parish of Cossall. After Cossall it was on to the parish of Trowell and again the lands of Lord Middleton and Isaac Pickthall. The next was the parish of Bramcote and the lands of John Sherwin and John Trowell. Then, once again, it was to pass through the lands of Lord Middleton in the parish of Wollaton. It's easy to see why he was so supportive of the canal from its inception.

The route of the canal approaching the town passed through the parish of Lenton and the lands of Mr Brentnall, Mr Millward and George DeLigne Gregory. The final section into Nottingham was through land owned by the Corporation, John Leaver, William Stanford and the Duke of Newcastle.

Water supply to canals was always of major concern to the engineers of the time, and the Nottingham was no different. This was made more of a worry due to the attitude of the Erewash Canal Co., who made sure no water was to be taken from their canal or any water supply to their canal; moreover, no water was to be taken from the parish of Wollaton or from the river Trent to feed the Nottingham Canal.

The Nottingham Co. were allowed to build reservoirs for water supply. These were to be built along the line of their canal with the exception of the one at Moorgreen. This was the largest of the reservoirs for which agreement was reached with the Cromford Canal Co., who insisted this be built before the junction of the two canals were made; the water would then enter their canal just north of the junction of the two canals before any water would be drawn

Nottingham Canal Co. seal, dated 1792. (Nottingham Historical Film Unit)

of by the Nottingham Co. These reservoirs were to be built at expense of the Nottingham Co.

No reservoirs, however, were to be built on land belonging to the Erewash Co. or on Lord Stanford's land. The Erewash Co. was allowed to take water from reservoirs belonging to the Nottingham and Cromford Cos. The Erewash Co. was also allowed to build reservoirs for its own use should the need arise, the cost of which was to be borne by the Nottingham Co. The Erewash Co. was determined to make it hard for the newly formed Nottingham Co., whilst safeguarding its own future. The Nottingham Co. was also not allowed to let any water off its top pound and was told it must keep a depth of no less than 3ft 6in. Any disputes between the companies were to be put to arbitration.

The Nottingham Canal was not to exceed 20 yards (18-28m) in breadth except where docks, wharves, basins or reservoirs were to be built. In Nottingham culverts were to be made under the canal for draining the parks owned by Henry Duke of Newcastle; these were to be made and kept in good repair at the expense of the canal company.

The Nottingham Canal Act allowed the company to raise £50,000 in the first instance (the estimate submitted by William Jessop having already been accepted). This was to be raised in £100 shares with no one shareholder allowed to hold more than ten shares. If a shareholder were to receive some shares by an Act of law or be left them in a will, these would be forfeit if there were more than ten in number. Each share would receive an interest of 5 per cent while the canal was under construction. All shareholders were to be allowed one vote per share for General Meetings and Special Assemblies.

If it was found that during construction the £50,000 was insufficient, the Act provided for a further £25,000 to be raised at £50 per share, making each share valued at £150. More could be raised by mortgage if required; the navigation would be put up as security. The interest on such a mortgage was to be paid half yearly in preference to the paying of dividends.

There did not appear to be any great difficulty in raising £75,000 for an undertaking such as the Nottingham Canal with the influential support it had. Of the £75,000 called in, made up of 500 £150 shares, £74,495 was actually paid in, the other £505 being default; this I believe was never paid in. It certainly had not been paid in by the time the balance sheet for 26 April 1797 came out.

The company's balance sheet for 16 February 1794 was as follows:

Paid to General Assembly.	£2,189 11s 8d (£2,189 58p)
Expense & General Committee Meetings	£77 14s 9d (£77 74½p)
Salaries	£552 10s (£552 50p)
Miscellaneous	£81 14s 6d (£81 72½p)
Interest	£1,655 17s 0p (£1,655 85p)
Canal & Works	£41,896 12s ¾ (£41,895 63½)
Purchase of Land	£100 (£100)

	£46,554 0s 5½d
	(£46,554 4½p)
In hand	£3,445 19 6½d
	(£3,445 5½p)
Total	£50,000 (£50,000)

The first general assembly of the Nottingham Canal Co. was held at the White Lion Inn, Nottingham, on 21 June 1792; all further general assemblies were to be held on the first Tuesday in May each year at 11 a.m. A special assembly could be called at any time for which at least ten days' notice had to be given. Each serving member of the committee was to have one vote, except for the chairman who would have the casting vote in the event of the votes being even.

Proper books and accounts were to be kept under the direction of the committee who had the power to call for the audit at any time and to settle outstanding accounts. All members of the committee were allowed a reasonable sum of money for expenses. They were also to have the power to purchase land, materials and all other items required for the works of the canal, to the drawing up of contracts for contractors working on the canal and the employing of clerks, servants, agents and workmen.

The committee, of course, had full power to make all the bye-laws for the navigation that they saw fit. The election of officers was to take place at the general assemblies for important positions such as chief clerk and treasurer, etc. All share money was to be called in as and when the committee agreed to do so; the first call had to be given ten days' notice, from which point further calls could be made at one month's notice. The amount of each call would probably be in units of £10.

The rates to be charged for some goods on the canal would have to be agreed with the Cromford Canal Co. These would be cargoes, which passed between the two canals. The Cromford Co. was not to take higher rates from the Nottingham Co. than it was taking from the Erewash Co. The Nottingham Co. could alter its rates at any general meeting or, if need be, call a special meeting, for which at least three months' notice must be given, the notice to be circulated to all members. Any reductions in the agreed rates would firstly be given to coal before any other merchandise.

The engineer William Jessop was unable to give all of his time to the one project, and had been ill at the time of the survey, so he recommended a very able young man by the name of James Green to assist him (James Green was a local man in the employment of Lord Middleton). He was, in the event, to spend far more time working on the construction of the canal than Mr Jessop himself.

The financial rewards for engineers like William Jessop could be enormous. Such engineers were at the top of their professions and very much in demand. A successful engineer would be working on a number of projects at the same time, which many of them did. It was also probable they would have shares in the various projects undertaken.

It was agreed at a committee meeting held at the White Lion Inn, Nottingham, on 26 June 1892 that William Jessop be the official engineer, James Green having previously been appointed to the position of superintendent of works for building the canal. This decision was taken at an earlier committee meeting on 28 January the same year. Jessop was retained at a fee of £3 3s (£3 15p) per day plus expenses. James Green was paid £315 per annum.

The canal company brought in some strict bye-laws for any misuse of the waterway. No boat was allowed to navigate the canal earlier than one hour before sunrise and no later than one hour after sunset without prior consent of the canal company in writing.

Boats were not allowed to moor overnight in the parishes of Trowell and Wollaton or in any place along the waterway where the embankment was more than 4ft (1,218m) in height above the level of the natural ground. The fine imposed for breaking either of the above bye-laws was £1 for the first offence and £2 for each subsequent offence.

Narrow boats, meaning boats with a beam of 6ft 10in (2,082m), should pass through locks side by side in order to save water; a fine of £1 would be imposed for not complying. I don't believe there would have been much revenue from this law as it was common practice for narrow boats to negotiate wide locks in this way.

Anyone leaving the towpath gates open would be fined £1 for each offence. Boats were not allowed to pass through the navigation on Sundays. All boats using the canal must show their name marked clearly on the side for identification. Pleasure boats were allowed to use the canal but should only be worked by sails or oars. Punts were not allowed as the poles could have damaged the bottom of the canal. A fine of £1 was payable for each of the above offences.

All lock gates had to be be opened before the boat was to enter a lock chamber; the reason for this was to prevent any damage to lock gates and stopping the practice of pushing lock gates open with the bow of the boat. Any damage done through not complying with this rule was to be compensated, plus a £2 fine. All the above bye-laws were passed at a general meeting held on 1 May 1804.

Further bye-laws were added which had been passed at a general meeting held on 6 May 1806. They were as follows: one of the company's collectors could stop any boat at any time to gauge it for weight and check the goods carried; no person was to damage the banks or fences along the side of the canal towpath; any person travelling along the towpath with a horse could not ride; anyone under the age of eighteen was not allowed to be in charge of a boat travelling along the navigation unless supervised.

One more law was added after the general meeting of 9 May 1807, which was to help save water: all boats using the navigation must give way to another boat at locks if that boat was nearest and the locks were in their favour. The distance was judged to be 150 yards. This must have been very difficult for the boatmen on the flight of locks at Wollaton where locks were very close together.

All penalties collected for misconduct were to be shared, half to the company and half to the informer.

It would appear from the dates these bye-laws came into force, that the company passed them after it was brought to their notice certain things were habitually being done which were undesirable and which could cause damage to the waterway. Changes would then be made at the general meetings held in May each year.

The canal company seal, dated 1792, was round, and approximately 1¾in in diameter. It figured a view of Nottingham Castle on the left and on the right the city with St Peter's church prominently situated on a hill. The canal was shown in the foreground with a boat passing along it.

2

CONSTRUCTING THE CANAL

Work started on the construction of the canal when the first sod was cut in July 1792, just six months after the Act received Royal Assent.

By September 1794, £140 of the share value had been called in, leaving only £10 per share remaining. The committee were getting concerned at the time it was taking. They considered the works were progressing too slowly; they had also expressed concern with the standard of some work carried out. So concerned were they that a letter was sent to Mr Jessop in October informing him of their reservations and stating they had very much hoped he would have given more of his time to their undertaking. Progress was not helped later the same year when the frost had been severe from late December to the middle of February 1795, followed by a rapid thaw causing terrible floods. These floods caused much damage to the canal at a time when most of the share money had been called in. The first 1½ miles into the city from the river Trent was open to the town wharves by July 1793, which would bring in a little welcome revenue.

Work also came to a stop for a time during the winter of 1793/94, when there was very bad weather. The ground was frozen for six to eight weeks; no work at all was done in that time. Mr Green, superintendent of works, was called in to report to the committee who were concerned about the stoppage. The long cold spell also caused damage to the waterway, which made repairs necessary.

The *Nottingham Journal* for Saturday 3 August 1793 hailed the opening of the first stretch of the Nottingham Canal:

On Tuesday last our canal (which is now made navigable up to the town from Trent Bridge) was opened for the reception of boats; on which occasion many thousand spectators assembled. In the first boat was the Engineer accompanied by an excellent band of music belonging to the Light Horse. The boats and were decorated with ribbons. At the filling of the first lock, the band played 'Rule Britannia' till the lock was full. In the course of the afternoon the first boatload of coal arrived, a wagon load of which was drawn by the boatmen through the principal streets and afterwards sold, the produce of which the boatmen had a drink (The Engineer who was in the first boat

General Statement of all the Accounts of the NOTTINGHAM CANAL COMPANY, to 26th April, 1797.

RECEIPTS.	£.	s.	d.
Of the Proprietors of the Canal, being £.150 on each Share deducting £.505 not paid	74,495	0	0
LOANS.			
Of the Proprietors Five Pounds on each Share, by Order of the Special Affembly of 28th January, 1796, deducting £.910 not paid:	1,590	0	0
Of feveral Proprietors as agreed upon at the General Affembly of 3d of May, 1796	1,110	0	0
Of Meffrs. Smalls	3,000	0	0
TOLLS, WHARFAGE, &c.			
To 11th April, 1796	153 13 10		
To 26th April, 1797	2270 14 6	2,430	8 4
BY INTEREST.			
For purchafe Money returned, Rent being agreed to be paid for the Land	129	3	4
	£. 80,754	11	8

DISBURSEMENTS.	£.	s.	d.
By Surveys, foliciting the Act of Parliament, &c. to 19th July, 1792	2,189	11	8
By Expences on General and Committee Meetings	228	19	11
By Salaries and Wages	1,750	17	10
By Intereft to the Proprietors, to 8th February, 1794	1,651	14	0
By ditto on Meffrs. Smalls Loan, to 20th April, 1796	104	10	4
By purchafe Money paid for Land	1,230	19	9
By the Canal and Works, Rents, and Damages	74,849	13	1
By fundry Payments in Meffrs. Smalls Accounts, including fome Rents and Compenfation for Damages	643	14	1
Balance in Hand	98	10	11
	£. 80,754	11	8

OUTSTANDING ACCOUNTS.

THE COMPANY Dr.	£.	s.	d.
	1,590	0	0
	1,110	0	0
To Meffrs. Smalls on Loan	3,000	0	0
To Intereft due to the Proprietors on the £.150 a Share, deducting for £.505 not advanced from 11th January to 26th April, 1796	7,510	0	0
	3,774	15	0
	375	10	0
To ditto on the Proprietors Loan of £.115,0 to 26th April, 1797	94	15	1
To ditto on Loan of £.1,110 to ditto	51	16	6
To a Year's Intereft of £.3,000 due to Meffrs. Smiths	150	0	0
TO BILLS OUTSTANDING TO REMAIN AT INTEREST.			
Mr. William Stretton for Toll-houfes, &c.	221 18 9		
Ditto for Houfes, Warehoufes, and Wharf	1,548 18 8	1,770	17 5
Mr. William Taylor for ditto		1,609	1 6
TO SUNDRIES.			
To a Year's Intereft on Mr. Stretton on £.221, and to Intereft to ditto on £.1,548 from 26th January, 1797, to 26th April		35	14 8
To Intereft on Mr. Taylor Loan in January, on £.1,699 to 26th April		27	0 11
To fundry Bills outftanding		837	13 10
To purchafe Money of Land, require to be paid		170	12 6
	£. 22,147	18	6

	£.	s.	d.
By Balance in Hand	98	10	11
By outftanding Debts due to the Company	33	13	-
By Part of the Calls not paid	505	0	0
Balance due from the Company on Accounts aforetained	21,807	14	6
	£. 22,147	18	6

N. B. The Amount of Debts due to the Owners of certain Collieries on the Line of the Canal from the Injury done by the Water of the Canal having flowed into the Collieries, and on outftanding Bills is not yet afcertained.

General statement of accounts for Nottingham Canal in 1797. (Nottingham County Library Local History Department)

would most probably have been James Green of Wollaton who was in charge of construction).

It was not officially completed until 1802, but the canal was open for traffic throughout its length in 1796. Most probably the work carried out after 1796 would have been on bridges, wharves, company warehouses and any other work, which could be left until after the navigation was complete. The navigation would take priority so that tolls could be collected from through traffic.

When the canal was officially completed in 1802 the total cost had mounted to a massive £80,000, which was a lot of money over 200 years ago. With the £75,000 called in from shares used, the company was able to raise the rest by mortgage, which the Act allowed for. A small amount of money was coming in from tolls taken from the bottom section in Nottingham, this being used whilst the remainder of the navigation was completed. It was the time of canal mania, when canals were being built in many parts of the country, many of them going over budget. This increase in expenditure was partly because in 1793 the country was at war with France; as a consequence of this the economy suffered rapid inflation leading to rising costs for canal builders.

The debts incurred by borrowing £5,000 on mortgage were finally paid off in 1804 and the company was able to pay its first dividend on shares in 1805. It was agreed by the company at a general meeting to limit the dividend to a maximum of 8 per cent per annum on each share, this being £12 on a £150 share to be paid in dividends of £6 twice a year in April and October.

It was a wide canal with nineteen locks and one stop lock. The stop lock was at the top end of the Nottingham Canal where it joined the Cromford Canal at Langley Mill. Lock sizes varied from 85ft long by 14ft 6in wide to 87ft by 15ft. The canal was 14¾ miles in length, the longest of a series of canals in the same area, all of which were completed about the same time and with the same dimensions.

All the locks on the Nottingham Canal (except for the stop lock) were in the first 5¼ miles of the canal's length, with Meadow Lane Lock being the first and also the entrance lock into the river Trent. The next lock up is Castle Lock and then Leather Mill Lock, which was just above the junction with the Beeston Cut. There were just two more locks at Radford Marsh before a flight of fourteen at Wollaton which took the canal to its summit level; these fourteen came close together, all within 2¾ miles. In these fourteen locks were two flights of three and a pair.

The locks were named as follows:

1   Trent (Meadow Lane) Lock
2   Castle Lock
3   Leather Mill Lock
4   Hicklings Lock
5   Simpsons Lock
6   Radford Bridge Lock
7   Lime Kiln Lock
8   Black Lock
9   (Bottom of first three)
10   (Middle of first three) First Flight
11   (Top of first three)
12   No name (known locally as Woodyard Lane Lock)
13   Blacksmiths Lock
14   (Bottom of top three)
15   (Middle of top three) Second Flight
16   (Top of top three) (Known locally as Coach Road)
17   Bottom of Woodend Lock
18   Top of Woodend Lock
19   Wollaton Lock (Top Woodend and Wollaton was a pair)
20   Langley Mill Stop Lock

See Appendix 1 for lock sizes, depth, rise and cubic capacity.

These locks varied in depth as did the amount of water needed to fill them. The least was 5,838 cubic feet and the greatest was 11,131 cubic feet.

The canal overflow weirs round the locks varied in construction, from some being open water channels to others taking the water underground round the side of the lock opposite the towpath. These weirs were essential to maintain the same water level throughout the canal. They were built about 12ft away from the lock-side, some were built of bricks and others with masonry stones. The masonry-built

Dried-up overflow weir above Lock No.15. These were very well built. The entrance was to the small tunnel that carried water from the weir underground round the lock to the pound below. This was 1977.

Overflow weir outlet from Lock No.17. At the time this picture was taken in 1976, it was possible to get through to the top end at the overflow above the top lock gates.

type was very well constructed. Where they entered the canal below the lock, the open water channel type ran over a lip into the canal; the underground type had two different kinds, a brick tunnel about 2ft diameter above water level and a masonry arch in the canal wall below water level.

From the original estimate submitted by William Jessop, it was proposed to build fifty-four bridges, twelve road bridges and forty-two occupation bridges. It

The flood level mark of 1852 can be found in the wall along the side of the towpath opposite London Road; the height of the mark would have meant most of the surrounding area was under several feet of water. This was taken in 1997.

seems that only thirty-six of the originally proposed number of fifty-four bridges were built throughout the length of the canal, nineteen of which were built from masonry stone or red brick, eight wooden swing bridges, two part red brick with a timber top, two wooden fixed bridges, one iron bridge, four not known. Of these thirty-six bridges, it is possible fifteen could have been road bridges. All bridges were attractive and well built, but alas, very few remain today. Of all the bridges constructed, only one was a change-over bridge, No.2, which changed the towpath from the right to left where it remained all the way to Langley Mill.

For details of the bridges, nos 1 to 36, from the river Trent upwards, see Appendix 2.

In conjunction with the Grantham Canal Co., the Nottingham Canal Co. built a wooden horse bridge across the river Trent, joining the mouths of both canals. This was to help speed up boat traffic between the two canals at a time when most boats were pulled by horses. This bridge survived until the 1860s when it was unfortunately washed away in a bad flood, never to be replaced. The two canals were by that time owned by the railways and traffic was falling off. The railways did not encourage canal traffic, as it would have been their responsibility to pay for the rebuilding of the bridge.

All materials for the construction of the canal were to be ordered through the company clerk, who in turn had to have the permission of the committee before releasing payments for these supplies if over the value of £10.

One of the most costly items during construction was for reservoirs for the much needed water supply. This was partly taken care of by building the top pound above Lock No.19 at Wollaton, 9½ miles long, which then also acted as a reservoir. With water supply always of a major concern to the canal engineer, it was important to find local streams and ponds which could be tapped into. There were eight water feeders, six feeding direct into the canal along its line and two joining together to enter the Cromford Canal just above its junction with the Nottingham Canal. Despite the early opposition from the Erewash Canal Co. the Nottingham Co. did manage to find water supplies in the area, all of which were

Above: Bridge No.1 showing the cast-iron cylinder installed to protect the bridge masonry against tow ropes in the days of horse-drawn boats. When first installed, it would have rotated when in contact with a rope. It has not moved for many years; this picture was taken in 1982.

Left: Bridge No.2 after the old hump-backed canal bridge was removed. It is the only change-over bridge on the canal; the towpath comes under the bridge on the left and back down on the right, where it remained all the way to Langley Mill. The Poplar Arm came in on the left, the towpath from under the bridge down the arm.

on the east side of the canal, except one. This last was from Wollaton, well away from the Erewash Canal, and water was also only taken from Nottinghamshire.

These feeders were:
Plantation
Shepherds Wood
Slave Plantation
Robbinetts

Giltbrook
Newthorpe Brook
Willey Spring
Nether Green Brook

Plantation feeder entered the canal above Lock No.6 in a 3ft. by 4ft (0.914m by 1.219m) culvert under the towpath at a point 3¾ miles from the river Trent. It was the only feeder entering the canal from the towpath side and was supplied from a pond at Wollaton. (This pond can still be found on Lambourne Drive, Wollaton, and is used by a local Angling Club.)

Shepherds Wood feeder entered the canal below Lock No.9, opposite the towpath coming from the direction of Bilborough.

Slave Plantation feeder entered below Lock No.11, opposite the towpath, also from the direction of Bilborough. (No trace of the two feeders from Bilborough can be found today.)

Robbinetts feeder entered the canal at the top of the so-named branch in a 2ft 6in by 4ft (0.762m by 1,219m) culvert coming from a pond in Oldmoor Wood, just to the west of Strelley village, Nottinghamshire.

Giltbrook feeder entered the canal at the top of the Greasley Branch, coming from the direction to the west of Hucknall, a town in north Nottingham-

The canal in 1921, with London Road on the left above the row of arches; the railings in the foreground were along the parapet of a towpath bridge that was the entrance to Sanitary Wharf for many years, used for the shipment of excrement from earth closets of Nottingham Tenement Courts.

London Road in 2004. Sanitary Wharf would have been on the right, opposite the boat travelling up the canal.

View down the towpath on London Road, taken in 1997.

shire, passing through Greasley and Giltbrook villages before reaching the canal.

Newthorpe Brook feeder entered the canal a little further up from the Greasley Branch, making its way to the canal via Eastwood, a town in east Nottinghamshire and the village of Newthorpe.

Willey Spring feeder made its way from Brinsley village west of Eastwood. It then joined Nether Green Brook before it entered the Cromford Canal above its junction with the Nottingham Canal. Nether Green Brook received its water supply from Moorgreen Reservoir.

To help with the carrying out of repairs along the canal, stop gates were fitted in the bridge entrances; these were very similar to the top gates of a lock, without the balance beam and winding gear. The paddle was operated with a hand pull attached to it and the operator would stand on the gate to pull the paddle up. Locks were fitted with stop plank grooves at the top and bottom of each lock for draining so repairs could be carried out.

From a report in the records of the Borough of Nottingham for Tuesday 3 November 1793, the Corporation were accused of interfering with the Nottingham Canal Committee and they had not removed a house known as Pinders House, which they had agreed to do. The house could have been in the way of the canal's construction as it was close to the canal's route through the town. It was agreed that the Corporation would receive two canal shares as compensation for the loss of the house.

The supply of materials was probably put out to local merchants, for them to deliver to where materials were required. Bricks would have been made locally and there were a number of brickworks around the area. Craftsmen were employed on a sub-contract basis, carpenters for lock gates and wooden swing bridges, and bricklayers for lock chambers, culverts and fixed bridges.

Cutters and diggers were employed for clearing the canal channel after which it would be lined with clay puddle; this would then be trampled into the canal bed with both men and horses. These men would most probably have been working on other canals and moved into the area when work started. Known as 'Navvies', short for Navigators, they would move on to another canal when the Nottingham Canal was finished. They would be paid for the amount of earth moved each day and would be the lowest paid. (These Navvies were well known for their drunkenness and bad behaviour, very often not turning up for work.)

The canal wall at the towpath side was built with large masonry stones; lock chambers seem to have been a mixture of masonry and brick with some all masonry. On the locks at Wollaton where they were built in flights, the pounds were short and built with masonry walls on both sides. This does not appear to have been common practice on all canals where flights of locks would have been built; it would also have been more costly.

3

BRANCHES AND WHARVES

Along the canal's line there were seven small branches and many wharves, most of the larger wharves being in Nottingham. Branches and wharves further up the canal out of Nottingham were mostly used for coal from local collieries.

From the bottom end of the canal in Nottingham, the first was the Poplar Branch, 2.2 furlongs long, followed by the Brewery Branch, 1.2 furlongs long, both completed in 1794. The Poplar Branch left the main line just west of Sneinton, heading west in that direction, while the Brewery Branch turned back in the direction of Nottingham, forming a loop back into the town. In 1836 the Poplar Branch was made longer by the addition of the Manvers Branch, which was 1 furlong in length; it was a private branch built by the Earl of Manvers, a very influential person in Nottingham at that time. He needed this branch to build his own wharves. By 1918 the Manvers Branch had been filled in and Manvers Street built over its course. All these three branches were approximately 1 mile up the canal from its junction with the river Trent.

The next branch, also in Nottingham, was the West Croft, for which the Act was passed in 1839; it was opened to traffic in 1842. This was the last branch to be built and had a short life, only being used for twenty-four years. It was also one of the first to be filled in and built over. It was half a mile in length and formed a loop, leaving the main line just below the Midland Counties Railway Station and re-entering the main line again near to Carrington Street. It was mainly used for coal wharves and was filled in by 1866, just twenty-seven years after receiving its Act, the Midland Railway Co. obtaining power to do so. What was the West Croft Branch is now under Platforms 4 and 5 of Midland Station, Nottingham, the station having been extended after the canal was filled in. On present-day street maps it would have been between Queens Road and Station Street, then turning sharply right and passing under Station Street before re-entering the main line.

Further up the canal at a point 5¼ miles from the river Trent came the Bilborough Cut; it was the longest branch along the canal and was 1 mile 5 furlongs long; it entered the main line above Wollaton top lock and terminated close to Bilborough Woods from where tramroads went up to both Bilborough

Silted-up Poplar
Arm close to the
junction with
the main line.
The towpath
was on the right;
the corrugated
bridge above the
canal was a link
between factories
on both sides. This
picture is from
1976.

and Strelley collieries. It was a private branch built at the expense of local landowners, and was also open to other users on payment of a toll. This branch was opened in 1799 but most of it was disused as early as 1813 with some parts filled in and it was totally disused by 1874. It would appear that once the two collieries had closed the branch had little use; today nothing can be found of either the two tramways or the Bilborough Cut.

After the Bilborough Cut, at 9 miles 7 furlongs, came the Robbinetts Branch; it was a short branch of only 3 furlongs long and was opened in 1796 to serve collieries to the east of the canal, to which tramways extended out. It leaves the main line just before it passes over the Cossall Embankment. On approaching this junction the branch carries straight on whilst the main line turns sharply to the left. Just one bridge passed over it, a wooden swing bridge at the beginning of the branch. It still contains water but there is no trace of the tramways that came down from the collieries.

The next and last branch was Greasley, at a point 11 miles 6 furlongs up the canal; it was just 1 furlong in length, and opened in 1800 to serve the collieries of the Duke of Rutland at Greasley and Fillingham, tramways connecting with both collieries from the waterway. There is nothing left of this branch or the tramways now; what was left after the canal had been abandoned would have been removed with the Shilo open-cast coal-mining operation.

Above: The Poplar Arm in 1997, now filled in, came in from the right. The buildings have also been demolished. The junction is now a winding hole.

Left: An old bollard on the towpath near to the new winding hole in No.12 Poplar Arm in 2004.

The canal near to the junction with the Poplar Arm and Hermit Street. The large factory, left, was Boots Pharmaceutical Ireland Factory, now demolished. Hermit Street is also no longer. Note the Trent Barge moored alongside the wharf on the right. This was 1921.

There were many wharves along the canal close to Nottingham. The first one was approximately half a mile from Trent Lock on the towpath side. A bridge carried the towpath over an entrance into this wharf. At the junction with the Poplar Branch, which comes in from the right, the next wharves were opposite the towpath just a short distance along from where the canal passed under London Road. These wharves were between Leen Side and Canal Street, which ran parallel with the canal; it is now all Canal Street. (In the 1790s it was half Canal Street and half Leen Side, Leen Side taking its name from the river Leen, which followed its original route through Nottingham at that time.) These wharves have now been filled in and built over; this has also happened to all the wharves opposite the towpath between Trent Street and Carrington Street.

There were a number of wharves on both sides of the canal between Carrington Street and Wilford Street. Once under Wilford Street and through Castle Lock, opposite the towpath, came Castle Wharf and Duke of Newcastle Wharf, both of which have now been filled in and built over. These wharves were between Canal and Castle Boulevard and at the side of Wharf Street.

Once out of Nottingham there were still a number of wharves along the canal, two on the pound in between lock nos 5 and 6. First came a wharf that later became known as Sanitary Wharf, located about 200 yards from Lock No.5. The second was a little further up this pound after a left turn and just before the canal turned right to pass under Radford Bridge. It was a coal wharf from Radford Colliery, served by a small tramway. Both these wharves were opposite the towpath.

Site of the Duke of Newcastle's Wharf. The entrance was between the buildings on the right. Nottingham Castle can be seen in the top left corner.

Hand-operated paddle in the stop gates at Swansea Bridge in 1976; the pull handle can be clearly seen. When maintenance was carried out requiring water to be drained from the canal, this paddle would be pulled up to allow water back in. The handle has since disappeared from the gate.

Gregory Street Bridge, Lenton, from a postcard taken in 1900; note Trent Barge through the bridge.

Just above Lock No.6 came the canal company's maintenance yard followed by a small wharf for some Lime Kilns above Lock No.7. There were no more until reaching Lock No.19 and a wharf for Wollaton Colliery. All of these have now long gone and there is no trace left of any of them. The one which remained the longest was the maintenance yard on the small pound in between lock nos 6 and 7. It was there until 1955 when it was filled in and piped, although it had not been used for many years.

There was a wharf for Cossall Brickworks, opposite the towpath just south of Awsworth. Also in this area, Babbington Colliery had a loading wharf with a tramway coming down from the colliery. There were also wharves at the top of both Robbinetts and Greasley branches.

Above: Boat yard on canal side at Lenton from a postcard taken in 1900; there is still a boat yard there today, named Trevithicks. They carry out boat repairs and maintenance.

Right: Early photograph of Nottingham Canal at Lenton, dated 1858. The place is not known but could be Gregory Street from the other side of the bridge.

Bridge over entrance to Castle Marina. Nottingham Canal is through the bridge.

4

ADMINISTRATION OF THE CANAL

The Nottingham Canal Co. appears to have had a good life, with trade being fairly brisk after a slow start, once the mortgage debt of £5,000 was paid off (required to finish construction, as mentioned earlier). A regular dividend was paid after 1805, nine years after the canal had opened to through traffic.

The main cargo carried was coal from collieries along the canal line, followed by iron, lime, limestone and manure with some farm produce. Most farm produce came from the Grantham Canal, a great amount of coal being sent in return.

In 1794 the company produced an estimate of what they hoped would be for goods carried and receipts taken.

The estimate was:

Estimated Goods carried & Receipts 6 March 1794

Coal 40,000 tons	Receipts £1,667	
Coal 20,000 tons (Nottingham only)	Receipts	£750
Lime	Estimated receipts only	£500
Wheat & Rye	ditto	£100
Stone	ditto	£210
Goods	ditto	£600
Bricks	ditto	£225
Coal via River Trent	ditto	£200
Total	£4,252	

This, however, did not materialise at a speed the company hoped for. It had still not reached the above estimate four years later at a committee meeting held on 25 April 1798. Receipts for the proceeding year were still over £1,000 down.

That statement was:
Receipts for year ending 25 April 1798
Tonnage of Goods   £2,614 5s 2¾d

Nottingham Canal Co. permit for the transportation of goods, made out to a G. Megson and dated March 1802. (Nottingham County Library Local History Department)

Tonnage Wharfage	£117 16s 9½d
Weighing Machine	£92 14s 10d
Land & Materials sold	£208 0s 10d
From Penalties	£2 15s 6d
Total	£3,134 3s 8¼d
	(£3,134 18p)

After paying dues for that year, only £54 15s 9d (£54 78p) was left in hand.

A good relationship between the Nottingham and Cromford Cos was maintained; they shared a tollhouse and toll collectors at Langley Mill where both canals joined. Competition was keen with the Erewash Co. In October 1797 a special toll of 3d per ton was introduced by the Nottingham Co. for coal travelling from Langley Mill to all points west of Beeston but this proved to be a financial disaster. The authorised toll was 1s (5p) per ton. In November the following year both Nottingham and Erewash companies agreed it was bad for trade, making an agreement not to offer inducements to collieries and to take full tolls on both canals, and also agreeing not to take trade from each other.

During its first years of trading the company was taking an average of £40 per week in tolls, making a yearly total of about £2,080, out of which they had to pay salaries, expenses and carry out repairs; when all these had been taken care of £1,200 was left. Of all tonnage carried during these early years, 90 per cent was coal and limestone.

In 1797 a package boat was running twice weekly for passengers between Nottingham and Cromford. The charge per trip was 5s (25p) for best cabin and 3s (15p) for second best. A further package boat was started a year later in 1798

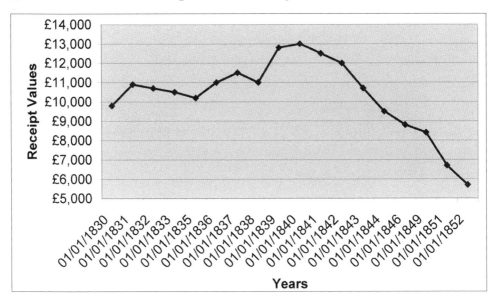

Graph showing tonnage carried between 1830 and 1852, the good years up to 1841 and the rapid decline between then and 1852 with the threat from railways.

from Nottingham to Leicester, charged at 5s (25p) first class and 2s 6d (12½p) second class.

By 2 May 1800 it was reported at the committee meeting that tonnage carried was 114,227 tons, of which coal accounted for 89,500 tons. Receipts had gone up to £4,647 6s 9¾d (£4,647 34p). It can be seen by the year 1800 that receipts were now £395 above what the estimate of 1794 had forecast, taking seven years. By year 1801, tonnage carried was once again improved, reaching 136,102 tons, coal again being its main cargo at 101,222 tons; of this 101,222 tons, 65,705 tons went down the river Trent and Grantham Canal. Trade was slow, however, through the Beeston Cut with less than 3,000 tons coming that way. Tolls had now reached £5,197 for 1801.

It is interesting to note that in 1796 when it was opened throughout its length, company accounts for April that year showed a total cost for canal and works of £78,800 6s ½d (£78,800 30p). As the undertaking was not officially completed until 1802 it is likely a little more was actually spent.

In the following year, 1797, accounts showed a total disbursement of £82,754 11s 8d (£82,754 58p) which included tolls, Wharfage interest and loans. Included also was money called in from shares out of a total of £75,000. Only £505 was not paid in, and just £98 10s 11¼d (£98 59p) was left for balance in hand.

Statement of Accounts for 6 April 1796:

Paid previously	£2,189 11s 8d	in £150 shares £75,000
Expenses general assembly	£184 8s 4d	Not in £505
Salaries	£1,329 4s	£74,435

Interest to proprietors	£1,651 14s	Loans	£3,000
Purchase of land	£1,233 12s 9d	Other loans	£1,590
Miscellaneous	£512 4s 11d	Tolls	£153 13s 10d
Allowance for interest	£7,100 15s 8d		

Total for Canal & Works	£78,800 6s	From Lord Middleton
Balance due to Company	£507 11s 1½d	£129 3s 4d
Total	£79,307 17s 2d	£79,307 17s 2d
(£79,307 76p)	(£79,307 76p)	

By 1830, when the canals were in their heyday, the Nottingham Co. was doing very well. Receipts had more than doubled; see the following list:

YEAR	RECEIPTS	
1830	£9,879 4s ½d	(£9,879 20p)
1831	£10,906 1s 10½d	(£10,906 09p)
1832	£10,621 19s 11½d	(£10,621 99p)
1833	£10,615 15s 7½d	(£10 615 78p)
1834	£10,015 1s 10d	(£10,015 09p)
1836	£10,776 17s 3½d	(£10,776 66p)
1837	£11,201 16s 10½d	(£11,201 84p)
1838	£10, 954 9s 4d	(£10,954 47p)
1839	£12,760 10s 1d	(£12,760 50p)
1840	£12,825 19s 10d	(£12,825 99p)
1841	£12,536 2s 9½d	(£12,536 14p)

By 1804, when the mortgage had been cleared, it was agreed at the annual general meeting to start paying a dividend of 8 per cent, £12 per £150 share. This was nine years after the canal was opened, putting payments nine years in arears – a situation which had only slightly improved when ownership was transferred to the railways. A last full payment was made in 1854 and should have been paid in October 1849. Dividend arrears had come down from nine years to five years. This improvement was brought about by sometimes paying three dividends in one year; normal dividends were paid in April and October. Years in which three dividends were paid were 1830, 1832, 1834 and 1845. These were not the only years that three dividends came out.

The following list gives dates of committee meetings at which it was agreed to pay the dividend (given in the first column), the date the dividend was due (in the centre), and the dividend paid (on the right). It can be assumed the dividend would be paid as soon after the committee meeting as it was convenient to do so.

Date Agreed	Date Due	Dividend
22 June 1829	April 1820	£6
2 November 1829	October 1820	£6

13 April 1830	April 1821	£6
22 September 1830	October 1821	£6
31 December 1830	April 1822	£6
3 May 1831	October 1822	£6
19 October 1831	April 1823	£6
7 February 1832	October 1923	£6
9 September 1832	April 1824	£6
19 December 1832	October1824	£6
17 April 1833	April 1825	£6
15 October 1833	October 1825	£6
16 January 1834	April 1826	£6
16 July 1834	October 1826	£6
3 December 1834	April 1827	£6
5 May 1835	October 1827	£6
28 October1835	April 1828	£6
24 February 1836	October 1828	£6
5 February 1845	October 1840	£6
7 August 1845	April 1841	£6
17 December 1845	October 1841	£6
7 August 1846	April 1842	£6
2 February 1847	October 1842	£6
29 June 1847	April 1843	£5

Lenton Chain junction of Nottingham Canal and Beeston Cut, Nottingham Canal turning off to the right, Beeston Cut coming from under the bridge on the left. The towpath was busy with children making their way home from school when this picture was taken in 1921.

The committee meetings and general assemblies were always very well attended. At these meetings it would seem that a different person would take the chair for a number of meetings in succession but no fixed number appears to have been laid down. One of the first to take the chair was Mr Joseph Oldknow, who as well as being an important man within the canal company, was also influential in Nottingham. Mr Henry Green, who was involved in the beginning when a canal was first promoted, followed him. Other people to take the chair at these meetings during the canal's sixty-three years of trading were Mr George Bott, Mr Thomas Hall, Revd Richard Alliott, Doctor Marsden, Alderman Wilson and Lord Middleton. (Lord Middleton was a member of the Willoughby family, he himself taking the name Middleton when he received his title of Lord.) Mr Thomas Bishop was one of the last to take the chair at meetings before the railway take over.

The main venue in Nottingham for both general assemblies and committee meetings was the White Lion Inn. The group did on some occasions use other inns in the city, including the Blackmoss Head Inn, George IV Inn, and Blackboy Hotel.

At its meetings the committee made all decisions, both large and small, regarding canal operations. It also carried out an annual survey of the waterway with regard to maintenance, a report being made note of at the first committee meeting after each survey.

One such survey report, made in 1834, reads:

Report Of Inspection 1834

Castle Lock new bottom gates.
Collectors House at Lenton to be repainted.
No.4 Lock repairs required.
No.5 Lock repairs required.
Repairs to towpath opposite Radford Coal Wharf.
No.9 Lock repairs tp gates, and also repairs to walls.
No.10 Lock repairs to lock and repointing.
No.11 Lock repointing.
No.12 Lock repointing.
No.13 Lock towpath repairs.
No.14 Lock repairs to lock side.
No.15 Lock towpath side repointing.
No.16 Lock top course repointing.
No.17 Lock lower side wall requires rebuilding.
No.18 Lock new wing wall at lock head.
No.19 Lock lower wing wall off side rebuild.

One more annual survey reported at a committee meeting held on 10 August 1836 was as follows:

Report Of Inspection 1836

Observed repairs to be carried out.

Radford Wharf, offside bank needs heightening also towpath.
Dock needs rewalling Radford Bridge.
No.6 Lock rebuilt.
Repairs to towpath walling between locks 6 and 7.
New stone weir Lime Kiln pound.
No.9 Lock offside needs repaving.
No.10 Lock repairs to lock head.
No.12 Lock repairs to lock.
No.19 Lock repairs to both sides.
New swing-bridge inspected.
Repairs to Hallams House and paint inside and out.

It would appear from these regular surveys that the canal was well maintained throughout its length. By comparing the two surveys, taken two years apart, nothing appears in 1836 that was in 1834, with the exception of repairs to lock nos 12 and 19, even then these repairs are not worded the same. Taking this into account, it would seem that repairs noted at these annual surveys were carried out.

At a committee meeting held earlier in 1830, on 7 July, after the annual survey report had been passed, it was ordered that Mr Henry Howell 'do immediately what is necessary for supporting of the canal bank at Cossall and repairing such parts as necessary due to recent damage from heavy rain'. Mr Howell was at that time superintendent of canal and works, a responsible position within the company; he was to hold this position for many years, at least until the railways took over. It would also be his responsibility to see that repairs laid down in the annual report were carried out. He was, however, still unable to purchase any materials or goods over the value of £10 without prior consent of the committee. This rule would probably have made his work difficult at times.

The company's first clerk was Mr Frances Evans, who worked in that capacity for many years. For some time the company offices were in Wheeler Gate, Nottingham, which changed to St Peter's Gate, Nottingham, in 1849 (the company's last office premises).

At a committee meeting held on 25 May 1829, it was agreed to pay Trent Navigation Co. £40 regarding a letter received from them requesting payment of their bill for £40 in respect of weighing and gauging boats. At this same meeting it was ordered that work should go ahead on the wall which was to be built between High Bridge Lenton and Derby Road Bridge. A further committee meeting held on 16 June 1832 ordered that Mr Henry Howell get the outside of the warehouse occupied by Samuel Hurst in Nottingham painted with lead paint.

On 16 June 1832, it was agreed by the committee to give permission to Nottingham Gas Co. to erect a suspension bridge over the canal, which they had requested earlier by letter. The bridge was to enable the gas company to reach land they had purchased on the other side of the canal. The gas company agreed to purchase land from the canal company on which to build their bridge at a cost of 14s (70p) per square yard. The piece of land was 25ft 6in long by 2ft wide, making the cost of this land

Lock No.3 at Abbey Bridge, Lenton. The bridge here used to be a hump back and was changed some time in the 1920s. The lock chamber was still in fine condition when this picture taken in the 1950s. (Nottingham County Library Local History Department)

£3 19s 2d (£3 96p). In this agreement the gas company were to build suitable walling on both sides of the bridge, to prevent coal and coke falling into the canal. It was necessary for bridge supports to stand on canal company land for which a rent of 1s (5p) per year was to be paid to the canal company.

With the committee being so heavily involved in all decisions regarding how everything was run within the company, they did at all times know what was going on and could pass this information to interested parties and shareholders.

The company had about twenty employees for most of the time, once trade had settled down, although it was cut back in later years in an effort to reduce costs. Those employed consisted of a company clerk, superintendent of works, two toll collectors, two masons, two lock keepers, two lengthmen, a blacksmith, a carpenter and a number of labourers. Wages were generally fair for the job done, rents for houses cheap and in some cases free. The company also gave an increase in wages over the years, for example as it did with toll collectors, who were being paid £1 per week in 1806, this rising to £1 15s (£1 75p) by 1835.

Wages paid to employees in the late 1830s:

Superintendent	Daily 6s 6d (32½p)	Weekly £1 13s (£1 65p)
Carpenter	Daily 5s 6d (27½p)	Weekly £1 8s (£1 40p)
Mason	Daily 4s 10d (24p)	Weekly £1 4s 2d (£1 20½p)
Blacksmith	Daily 4s 6d (22½p)	Weekly £1 2s 6d (£1 12½p)
Labourer	Daily 4s (20p)	Weekly £1 (£1 00p)
Lock Keeper	Daily 3s 9d (18½p)	Weekly £0 18s 9d (£0 93½p)

The above wages were before drastic cuts in 1844 and 1849 made to reduce costs against railway competition.

With some of these positions also came rent free housing, while others were given free ale. Two toll collectors, as stated earlier, were employed with the company; it

Taken in 1976 from near same the position as the previous picture, the lock chamber and gates have been removed and the canal bed used to carry the re-routed river Leen on its way to the river Trent. The remains of the canal towpath can be seen under the bridge on the right.

was a good job which required a trustworthy person. Temptation was easy in this kind of work, hence the reason for a fair wage. A toll collector was not allowed to trade with boat people so as not to show favours to any boat owners. The two toll offices I remember were situated on the opposite side to the canal towpath, one on the length of canal between lock nos 4 and 5 at Radford Marsh, a second at the head of the canal where it joined with the Cromford Canal at Langley Mill. This office was shared by both companies.

Most trade was done for cash, with one exception: some boats travelling through the canal could get up to three months' credit if they used the waterway regularly. This probably was allowed so as to encourage regular return traffic.

In later years the famous canal carriers Fellows, Morton & Clayton Ltd had their wharves and warehouses for a time on Canal Street, Nottingham.

There seems to have been a steam packet boat operating on the canal by Messrs Hooton and Bradshaw. They were successfully prosecuted in January 1826 for operating on the canal, which was in violation of a decision passed at a committee meeting held in May the previous year, 'not to allow Steam Packet vessels to pass with engine at work'. They protested against the ruling, at a committee meeting of May 1826, where it was agreed to allow passage at the companies discretion.

In March 1832 Mr German Wheatcroft asked for permission for his flyboats to pass through the locks at all hours. He was trying to promote new trade from the High Peak Railway, which had a terminus at the head of the Cromford Canal and another terminus at the other end of its line with the Peak Forest Canal, which would give a route into Manchester via its link with the Ashton Canal. Traders on other canals were now allowed to pass at all hours.

5

THE DECLINING YEARS

With the coming of the railways, the threat to trade became very real. It did not take long before the Nottingham Canal Co. began to have a drop in trade; they started to feel the pinch in 1843, with a slow fall continuing. Things got worse as years passed, with receipts almost halved in a decade. It was, however, not alone in this experience, for many canal companies all over the country were being seriously affected in the same way.

The following list shows how receipts were to fall from 1841 to 1852:

YEAR	RECEIPTS
1841	£12.536
1842	£12.184
1843	£10.761
1844	£9.443
1846	£8.965
1849	£8.536
1851	£6.745
1852	£5.981

In 1844 tolls were reduced and staff dismissed from employment in an effort to economise; some privileges, previously given for many years, such as free beer and house rent, were taken away.

Further cutbacks were made in late 1849 after a committee meeting held on 7 November of that year. Mr Henry Howell, superintendent of works, was to prepare a report to submit to the committee on the proposed reduction of expenditure. His report showed a saving of £284 per annum. The saving was on day wages at £180 with a further £104 in other labour costs. It was accepted by the committee, with a possible future reduction in salaries of toll collectors, which would be looked into at a later date. The committee turned down an application from Mr Samuel Hurst for a reduction in rent on his warehouse at the same meeting. Also agreed to at the same meeting was that coal and coke carried down the river Trent to Torksey Lock would be charged at 6*d* (2½p) per ton.

Mr Howells report was as follows:

NAME	WORK	DAY RATE	RENTS
Mr Howell	Superintendent	5*s* (25p)	20 per cent per annum
Mr Parkin	Carpenter	4*s* (20p)	2 per cent per week
Mr Draper	Blacksmith	3*s* (15p)	20 per cent per annum
Mr Wade	Mason	3*s* 4*d* (16½p)	20 per cent per annum
Mr Cordin	Labourer	2*s* 6*d* (12½p)	
Mr Taylor	Lock Keeper	2*s* 3*d* (11p)	
Mr Stanton	Labourer	2*s* 3*d* (11p)	
Mr Wallis	Labourer	2*s* 6*d* (12½p)	5 per cent per annum
Mr Lyson	Labourer	2*s* 6*d* (12½p)	20 per cent per annum

Salaries were also cut, these being staff personnel such as company secretary; office staff and toll collectors would have probably received reductions later. Salaried employees do not appear to have been as badly affected as daily rate workers.

It was understandable that the company should make every effort to reduce costs with the difference between receipts and wages getting smaller year after year. The following list gives receipts of four different years against wages, salaries and profits. The best example is the difference between 1841 and 1851 which shows receipts down by almost half, wages and salaries cut by just over one third, and profits down by just over half. I have rounded the figures to pounds only.

Year	Receipts	Wages	Salaries	Profit
1829	£9,425	£912	£435	£8,078
1841	£12,536	£1,099	£522	£10,915
1851	£6,745	£468	£535	£5,742
1852	£5,981	£468	£447	£5,066

As early as 1830 it was thought there could be a threat to trade when a railway line was proposed from Cromford to Leicester. The Nottingham Co. co-operated with the Loughborough and Leicester navigations in opposing the line. This threat increased in 1836 with the formation of Midland Counties Railway who opened two lines in 1839 from Nottingham to Derby and Nottingham to Leicester. This company later amalgamated with others to form Ambergate, Nottingham, Boston & Eastern Junction Railway Co.

With the railway threat imminent, it did not help the canal company; some of its directors were on the committee of both railway and canal companies. The Nottingham Canal Co., seeing the writing on the wall (as the saying goes), decided it would be better to sell out to the railways rather than try to fight them.

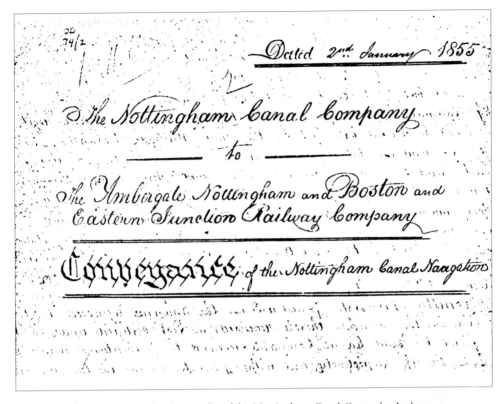

Above and below: Documents for the transfer of the Nottingham Canal Co. to the Ambergate Nottingham Boston & Eastern Junction Railway Co., dated 2 January 1855. (Nottingham County Library Local History Department)

ANNO NONO & DECIMO

VICTORIÆ REGINÆ.

✻✻

Cap. clv.

An Act for making a Railway from or near the *Ambergate* Station of the *Midland* Railway, through *Nottingham*, to *Spalding* and *Boston*, with Branches therefrom, and for enabling the Company to purchase the *Nottingham* and *Grantham* Canals.   [16th *July* 1846.]

WHEREAS the making of a Railway from the *Midland* Railway in the Parish of *Crich* in the County of *Derby*, through *Nottingham*, to *Spalding*, with an Extension of the said Railway diverging from the Main Line thereof in the Parish of *Pickworth* in the Parts of *Kesteven* in *Lincolnshire* to the Town and Port of *Boston* in the same County, and a Branch Railway diverging from the Main Line of Railway in the Parish of *Welby* to the Town of *Slenford* in the Parts of *Kesteven* in *Lincolnshire*, would be of great public Advantage: And whereas the Persons herein-after mentioned are willing, at their own Expence, to carry such Undertaking into execution: And whereas an Act was passed in the Thirty-second Year of the Reign of King *George* the Third, intituled *An Act for making and maintaining a navigable Canal from the Cromford Canal in the County of Nottingham to or near the Town of Nottingham, and, to the River Trent near*

[*Local.*]   32 M   *Nottingham*

Right and below: The Act for building a railway
with branches from Ambergate through
Nottingham and enabling the company to
purchase both Nottingham and Grantham canals,
dated 16 July 1846. (Nottingham County Library
Local History Department)

9° & 10° VICTORIÆ, *Cap.*clv.

SCHEDULE.

—————

Form of Conveyance of Canal.

THIS Indenture, made the   Day of   184 ,
between the Nottingham Canal Company, *or the Company of
Proprietors of the* Grantham Canal Navigation, of the one Part, and
the Ambergate, Nottingham, and Boston and Eastern Junction
Railway Company of the other Part, witnesseth, That the said
Nottingham Canal Company [*or the Company of Proprietors of the
Grantham Canal Navigation*], in consideration of the Sum of
to them paid by the said Ambergate,
Nottingham, and Boston and Eastern Junction Railway Company,
the Receipt whereof is hereby acknowledged [*or* (*if the Case be so*)
in consideration of   Shares in the Capital
Stock and Property of the said Ambergate, Nottingham, and Boston
and Eastern Junction Railway Company], appropriated by the said
Railway Company to or for the Use and Benefit of the Proprietors
of the Nottingham Canal Navigation [*or the Company of Proprietors
of the Grantham Canal Navigation*], the Appropriation of which
Shares is hereby acknowledged, *or* (*if the Case be so*) in consideration of the Sum of   and of
Shares in the Capital Stock and Property of the said Ambergate,
Nottingham, and Boston and Eastern Junction Railway Company,
paid and appropriated respectively by the said Railway Company,
to and for the Use and Benefit of the Proprietors of the said
Nottingham Canal [*or the said Company of Proprietors of the
Grantham Canal Navigation*], the Receipt and Appropriation
whereof respectively are hereby acknowledged, and, by virtue and
in pursuance and under the Authority of the said Ambergate,
Nottingham, and Boston and Eastern Junction Railway Act, One
thousand eight hundred and forty-six, do hereby convey all that the
navigable Canal called the Nottingham Canal [*or the Grantham
Canal Navigation*], with the collateral Cuts, Towing Paths, Works,
Hereditaments, and Appurtenances thereto belonging, and all the
Powers and Authorities vested in the said Nottingham Canal Company [*or the Company of Proprietors of the Grantham Canal
Navigation*], for maintaining the said Canal [*or Canal Navigation*]
and Premises, unto and to the Use of the said Ambergate, Nottingham, and Boston and Eastern Junction Railway Company, absolute'y
and for ever, but subject to all existing Liabilities and Restrictions
affecting the same Canal [*or Canal Navigation*] and Premises,
and subject also to the Provisions of the said Ambergate, Nottingham, and Boston and Eastern Junction Railway Act; and the said
Ambergate, Nottingham, and Boston and Eastern Junction Railway
Company

Company do hereby accept and take the said Nottingham Canal
Navigation [*or the said Grantham Canal Navigation*] and Premises,
subject to the Liabilities and Restrictions aforesaid, and to the
Provisions of the Railway Act aforesaid.   In witness, &c.

——————

LONDON : Printed by GEORGE E. EYRE and WILLIAM SPOTTISWOODE,
Printers to the Queen's most Excellent Majesty. 1846.

In their case, the railway company was the Ambergate & Manchester Railway Co. They were to purchase the Nottingham Canal Co. at an agreed price of £225 for each canal share and to keep the canal in good order and repair. In this agreement made between the two companies, it stated the railway company should complete the purchase of the canal company at its agreed price no later than six months after the first section of railway was opened. This would probably mean its line between Ambergate and Nottingham.

The Ambergate & Manchester Railway Co. received its Act as early as 16 July 1846, at which time it was officially agreed to purchase the Nottingham Canal.

Shortly after this, the Ambergate & Manchester Railway Co. was itself to amalgamate with two other railway companies, The Nottingham, Vale of Belvoir & Grantham Railway Co. and The Nottingham & Boston Railway Co. These three companies changed their names to become one new company, The Ambergate, Nottingham, Boston & Eastern Junction Railway Co.

It turned out that after the amalgamation of the three railway companies, the first part to be opened was from Nottingham to Grantham in July 1850. Six months after the opening, as agreed, the Nottingham Canal Co. together with the Grantham Canal Co. applied to the railway company for the official takeover, which had been agreed earlier with the Ambergate & Manchester Railway Co. (the Grantham Canal Co. having made its own agreement with the railway companies). But the railway companies refused, negotiations took place without any success and they still refused to pay. Both canal companies then took out an injunction against the railway company, which took several court cases and a lot of expense and which did, in fact, go all the way to the House of Lords.

At a committee meeting held on 19 October 1854, it was agreed that £2,000 of £3,000 of costs at law received be paid by the Grantham Canal Co. This had been decided earlier at a conference held with the Grantham Canal Co. committee on 4 September 1854. Also, two thirds of any balance due was to be paid by the Grantham Co. and one third by the Nottingham Co. It would seem that both companies had made provision to set aside £4,000 for these costs; the remaining £1,000 was to be paid towards their own Parliamentary expenses. Any further expenses possibly incurred were to be paid equally by each company.

At the final committee meeting of the Nottingham Canal Co., held on 4 April 1856 (just sixty years after the canal was opened throughout its length), the accounts having been finally audited, it was agreed to pay a final dividend of £1 10s (£1 50p) per share, and also to go ahead with the sale of the canal to the Ambergate, Nottingham, Boston & Eastern Junction Railway Co. The conveyance for transferring canal to railway was completed and signed by three members of Nottingham Canal Management Committee on 2 January 1855; these members were Mr William Bishop, Mr William Hanney and Mr Thomas Hopkins.

The £225 which had been agreed as payment for canal shares with the Ambergate & Manchester Railway Co. before it amalgamated with other companies to form the Ambergate, Nottingham, Boston & Eastern Junction Railway Co. was not paid in full as a cash payment. Only £50 in money was paid for each share, making a total payment of £25,000 for all 500 shares. Balance was accepted in railway shares, a total of £87,500 in 500 shares valued at £175 each; each share was numbered from 751 to 1,250 inclusive, and dated 30 October 1854.

The canal did not remain under ownership of the Ambergate, Nottingham, Boston & Eastern Junction Railway Co. for long, when they changed to become Nottingham, Grantham Railway & Canal Co. This was later to become part of the Great Northern Railway Co. in 1861.

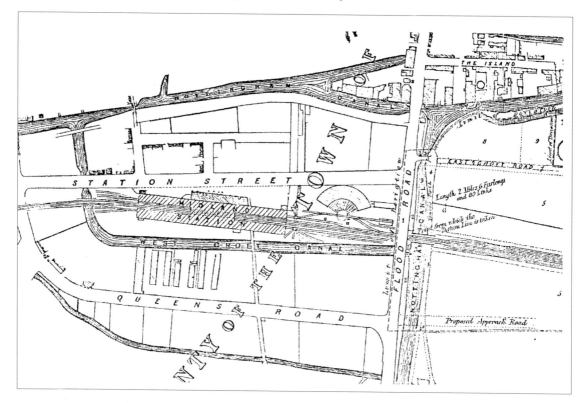

Portion of plan deposited at Parliament by the Ambergate, Nottingham, Boston & Eastern Junction Railway on 30 November 1853, showing the plan for Nottingham Midland Station. It also shows the West Croft Canal, filled in when the station was built. (Nottingham County Library Local History Department)

Traffic was down to 123,488 tons by early 1900s, most of this being carried on the bottom section to warehouses between Lenton and the river Trent. Some still came through the Beeston Cut. Most of this traffic also came down the Trent from Loughborough and Leicester via the Soar Navigation (now the Grand Union Canal). A small amount was still travelling the full length from Cromford; both Radford and Wollaton coal wharves were still in use and sending some coal into Nottingham.

Part of the reason for a fall in trade was that railway companies did nothing to encourage traffic on canals, preferring to get as much as possible on the railways. By 1916 receipts were down to £1,028, tons carried down to 96,686, of which merchandise was 31,887 tons, the largest commodity, followed by coal at 17,133 tons, gravel at 16,819 tons, road stone at 16,116 tons and manure at 14,731 tons.

By this time the canal was suffering from poor maintenance and neglect, especially in the top reaches and heavily locked section at Wollaton, due to little repair over the years. There were complaints about lack of water in some parts, mainly above Lenton, but the Great Northern Railway, who still owned the canal at that time, did nothing to improve conditions, which slowly worsened.

The Trent Navigation Co., the largest trader using the canal, was suffering due to the canal's lack of depth and the poor maintenance of the canal. Several

Above left: Re-routed river Leen following the course of the canal just above Lock No.3, which was just round the left bend at the centre of the picture, taken in 1976.

Above right: Bricked-up entrance to Bridge No.9 at Derby Road, Lenton, in 1977; this bridge was just a short distance from the bottom entrance to Lock No.4.

The canal at Hillside off Derby Road, Lenton; this section of canal is now used by the re-routed river Leen. The date is unknown. (Nottingham County Library Local History Department)

Acts were passed to improve the navigation and increase tolls. An Act of 1858 allowed tolls to be increased, but in 1869, due to a decline in trade, they had to be reduced again. In the 1930s attempts were made to improve both Beeston Cut and Nottingham Canal, but these also fell through. In 1936 the London & North Eastern Railway Co., now the owners, let the canal to Trent Navigation Co.

The last traffic through the canal above Lenton was in 1928; a fair amount of traffic was still using wharves in Nottingham with a little through Beeston

The long parapet above of Bridge No.9 at Derby Road, Lenton, still intact in 2004. To the left of the line of white posts are the old gates to Wollaton Park.

Hicklings Lock No.4 at Radford Marsh. Lock No.5 bottom gates can be seen above the group of people on the left. This was 1925. (Nottingham County Library Local History Department)

Cut. The canal was officially abandoned above Lenton Chain in 1937. With the bottom 2¼ miles now in the hands of the Trent Navigation Co., they had control of the 4½-mile waterway from Beeston Lock to the river Trent. This stretch of waterway remained in their ownership until 1948 when it came under British Transport Commission. The last and present owners are British Waterways, who took over from British Transport Commission in 1963. It was then that the canal came back into the ownership of one company again after it was separated when Trent Navigation Co. acquired the Nottingham section.

One other change took place in 1977 when Broxtowe Borough Council purchased the top section, a 6-mile stretch of the top pound from Bramcote passing through Trowell, Cossall, and Awsworth to Eastwood. It was declared a Local Nature Reserve in 1993 and now offers a refuge for wildlife, also providing a public amenity for walkers, cyclist, naturalists and in some areas horse riders and anglers. The council provides information packs giving details of circular walks with historic notes and natural attractions along the canal. Car parks for visitors are available at Cossall and Awsworth, with limited parking available at a number of other locations. Although Broxtowe Borough Council owns the canal, it receives assistance in managing it from Nottinghamshire Wildlife Trust, The British Trust for Nature Conservation Volunteers, The Countryside Agency,

Nottinghamshire County Council and Awsworth Angling Club. Since the canal's main water supply at the Great Northern Basin was severed a number of years ago, much of the council's work has involved trying to make best use of the water available and where possible provide new supplies. Areas have been dredged and ponds formed to try to maintain areas of open water and a mix of wetland habitats. The construction of the Awsworth Bypass in 1995 provided an opportunity for improved water supply by directing rainwater into culverts down to the canal. This, along with provision of an electric pump in 1998 to abstract water from the river Erewash, now means that even in the driest conditions some of the wetland areas can be maintained. The canal's towpath and bridleways connecting to the towpath were dedicated as public rights of way in 1998. Nottinghamshire County Council assists Broxtowe Borough Council with improving these routs where possible to a standard whereby those with disabilities can gain access. It can be seen that the canal's function in this area has changed over the years but remains a popular public amenity and important wildlife site in the Erewash Valley.

In the early 1800s, before the intervention of railway competition, the canal had a major role in development of industry in the Nottingham area. Coal became much cheaper, as we already know, coming down to the many wharves. A lot of small industries were soon to be built very close to the canal.

After the top section of the canal, above Lenton Chain, was abandoned in 1937 nothing happened to it for about eighteen years. Left to deteriorate, some parts became very shallow, mostly in the lower reaches.

The towpath was always kept clear even though the hedge was rather high in places. It was well walked, mostly at weekends. Fishermen (including myself) used it regularly, but mainly above Lock No.8; below this point one very rarely saw anyone fishing. Wollaton Colliery was still using the canal for depositing wastewater from the pit baths at this time.

The canal did not escape the Second World War without a little damage. In April 1941 it was hit during an air raid on Nottingham by a lone German bomber, who at the time seemed to have been trying to bomb the railway line on a clear moonlit night. He flew down the railway line, which is fairly straight at this point, releasing his bombs. Fortunately, the railway survived. Charlbury Road, Nottingham, runs parallel here with the canal on one side and railway on the other. Houses back onto one side of the canal and railway the other. Of the bombs released, some fell on houses in Charlbury Road, destroying them and killing some of the occupants, while others fell on the opposite side of the railway destroying houses in Felstead Road. Of the rest, some fell in Browns Woodyard near to Woodyard Lane, Wollaton, which is on the far side of the canal away from Charlbury Road. The last one fell in the canal, I believe in the pound between lock nos 8 and 10. It did not do much damage; if I remember correctly, this bomb did not go off. At the time of this bombing I was living with my parents close to the railway line and the blast from these bombs blew out some windows in our house.

It was in later years, during the 1950s, when the canal started to disappear above Lenton Chain to well above Wollaton. The filling in of this stretch of canal took

Left: Simpsons Lock No.5 at Radford Marsh. The wall to the left of the lock was the old Wollaton Park boundary; it was obviously a good place for swimming when this picture was taken in 1919.

Opposite above, left: The canal being filled and piped at Radford Bridge Road at the pound between lock nos 6 and 7. Lock No.7 can be seen behind the crane in the canal bed. This was taken on 9 August 1955. (Nottingham County Library Local History Department)

Opposite above, right: Bottom entrance to Lock No.6 in 1976. The left side bottom entrance wall with number plate is all that remains, the canal bed was filled in to towpath level and used as an underpass to the road.

Lock No.6, Radford Bridge. When this picture was taken in 1921, both bottom gates were open giving a view down the lock to the top gates.

Right: Jackie Mathew's
farm stands on land
between Radford Bridge
Road and the course
of the canal, which had
a small wharf between
lock nos 7 and 8. The
house still remains but
without the canal.

place over a number of years, starting in 1955 when it was drained and piped
from Derby Road, Lenton to Radford Bridge Road, close to Radford–Wollaton
border. This involved moving lock chambers 4 & 5 at Radford Marsh. This work
carried on for a number of years up until 1962, by which time the canal had
been piped and filled up to Lambourne Drive, Wollaton, lock chambers 6 to 12
had been removed, half of the Wollaton flight. The actual draining of this section
from Lock No.6 took place in two operations, the first between 14 and 29 July,
the second between 5 and 18 August 1959. The work probably lasted so long
due to the laying of pipes in the large canal bed, all the pipe laying needing to
be completed before it could be connected to the main sewer system. When the
piping and filling in was completed up to Lambourne Drive, Wollaton, Lock
No.13 was built in with a sloping brick front in the position of the top gates, both

Lock No.9 bottom lock in the first flight of three, still in fine condition in 1953 when this picture was taken. The line of houses accompanying the canal are on Charlbury Road. Note the telegraph poles; these also accompanied the canal for a few miles. (Nottingham County Library Local History Department)

Woodyard Lane Bridge. Lock No.13 bottom gates are visible through the bridge, seen here in 1919 on a calm day.

gates having been removed. This brick slope was fitted with a grill about 3ft 6in (1,072m) high from the base of the wall. The grill was approximately 2ft (0,608m) square; this would allow water into the lock chamber while keeping a depth of water in the canal above this point. The top of this lock chamber was built over with concrete and fitted with three inspection covers forming what can only be

Above: Taken thirty-four years later in 1953, this scene at Woodyard Lane has changed very little. The canal does appear more silted up.

Left: Blacksmiths Lock No.13 with two empty narrow boats travelling up in the direction of Wollaton. This was taken in 1918.

Lock No.13 in 1976; the top entrance had been built with a wall sloping backwards. In the top gates in the centre was a grill, to allow water to run into the lock chamber should it reach that height. The canal above here remained in water for a few more years. The lock chamber was turned into a very large type manhole with inspection covers at the top. Below, it had been piped in 1955.

Woodyard Lane as it appeared in 2004; the canal would have crossed close to where the lamp-post is on the right.

This pond on Lambourne Drive, Wollaton, known as Plantation, was used for water supply to the canal, entering in a culvert under the towpath above Lock No.6 at Radford Bridge. This view was taken in 1996. The pond is now used by fishermen.

described as a very large manhole, being approximately 14ft 6in (4,42m) wide and 80ft (24,24m) long. This now formed the entrance to the piped section, above which the canal remained untouched and full of water for a few more years.

From Lambourne Drive, the position of this now very unusual lock chamber upwards to Wollaton Colliery was drained on 29 August 1966. That included all the remaining locks up to No.19, the top lock. It was probably left in water longer because Wollaton Colliery was still in use until the end of 1963, when it officially closed for production. It remained open for a further nine months whilst machinery was removed. The canal was probably in water along this section, the colliery still using it for disposing of its waste water. This water was not dirty, but clean and warm, coming from the colliery baths. As I said earlier, we used it for swimming and never came to any harm.

Part of the top pound from Wollaton to Trowell seems to have been drained even earlier, on 23 September 1964. Further up on the top pound in the area of Awsworth and almost to Bailey Grove a great section of canal disappeared with the progress of open-cast coal mining. This, of course, completely removed all trace of the canal. The coal companies at that time were not obliged to replace the line of canal once coal had been taken out. When grass, trees and shrubs have grown back over the land again, it will doubtless look similar to how it did just over 200 years ago.

A tree growing out of the canal wall in the pound between lock nos 14 and 15, in 1977.

Looking down the canal in the direction of Lock No.1; top lock gates can be seen in the centre with the lock house to the right. British Waterways' facilities are on the left close to the second boat down. This was taken in 2004 from where factories once stood.

The apartments that replaced the factories above Lock No.1, taken in 1997 from the towpath.

Above: Remains of the water intake above the lock gates on the right side at Lock No.15 in 1996.

Right: Lock No.16, the top of the second flight of three, taken from Coach Road Bridge in November 1953. Everything looks in fine condition sixteen years after abandonment. Lock No.17 is in the distance.

Oval-shaped pound between lock nos 15 and 16. The canal walls are in good condition, the overflow weir in the wall to the right. The break in wall on the left was the entrance to Coach Road Bridge. Lock No.16 was through the bridge; gates can be seen over the bank. This was taken in 1961. (Peter Stevenson)

The same pound as on the previous page, between lock nos 15 and 16, taken from Lambourne Drive, Wollaton, in 2004, this time looking in the opposite direction. The canal walls are still intact.

Arched overflow weir outlet in the canal wall of the pound between lock nos 15 and 16, 1976.

6

THE LAST
THIRTY YEARS
FROM 1970

The inaugural meeting of the Nottingham Canal Society was held at Wollaton Village Church Hall, Bramcote Lane, Wollaton, on Thursday 22 July 1976. The purposes of the society were as follows:

1. To stimulate public interest and appreciation of the beauty, history and structure of the canal.
2. To promote the restoration of the canal between Langley Mill and Coventry Lane, Nottingham for the purposes of recreation and navigation.
3. To promote the preservation of the whole of the remaining areas of the canal for their use and enjoyment by the public.

Between forty and fifty people attended the meeting to hear the ideas put forward. The meeting lasted one hour twenty minutes, with many questions being asked, mostly about the practicalities of restoration. A ten-member committee was set up to look at a constitution, and it was decided to have a restoration feasibility study carried out and a corresponding report taken back to another public meeting by September. Assurances were given at the meeting that there would be no conflict of interest between the society and Broxtowe District Council – it was known at the time the council had shown an interest in purchasing a length of canal agreed at a meeting held on 15 May 1974, with the view to making picnic areas with car parking available. This could have meant filling in some sections and at the same time the cleaning out of others, after which the cleaned out sections would be re-watered and stocked with fish. Fishing rights could then be discussed with interested Angling Societies at a later date. The area discussed was, at the time, a 5-mile section of canal north of the B6004 road, north of Trowell.

The new society hoped to achieve, through talks with interested parties, a declaration of intent not to destroy any further lengths of canal and, in the case of open-cast coal mining, some promise of restoration afterwards. One of the first hopes was for volunteers to give the canal the facelift it badly needed in many

Above left: Rubbish-filled entrance at the site of Coach Road Bridge, Wollaton, taken in 1976.

Above right: Lock No.17 Bottom Woodend, full of rubbish; the walls are in excellent condition and the remains of top gates can still be seen after its being set on fire. This was taken in 1976.

Top entrance to Lock No.17 taken from the canal bed in 1976. Note the height of the canal walls; they give a good idea to the depth of water in the canal. Houses on Torvill Drive, Wollaton, have been built over this area.

Above: Bottom of second flight of three. Lock No.14 is on the top right side, showing the lock sill with a ground paddle inlet above and outlet below. This was taken in 1976.

Left: Lock No.18, the top of Woodend, showing the bricked-up bottom entrance in 1976. This lock has been built over by housing on Torvill Drive, Wollaton.

places; it was felt that residents of nearby villages of Trowell, Cossall and Awsworth would much prefer an attractive amenity to an untidy eyesore.

Broxtowe District Council followed up the May meeting with one held on 16 October the same year, at which proposals were discussed with Nottingham and Beeston Canal Association, regarding developing both waterways for amenity use. One of the main subjects discussed was the making of the towpath into a public right of way. Also on the agenda for discussion was the use of volunteer labour for some work, this being readily available. Nothing appears to have resulted from this meeting. According to a report in the *Nottingham Weekly Post*, Issue No.298 for 22 January 1976, plans were unveiled for a 'Canal Walk' along the towpath from Meadow Lane, Nottingham to Beeston. These plans were to improve the appearance of the canal bank and to make the towpath a public right of way; Nottinghamshire Leisure Services Committee approved them in principle. The British Waterways Board has an agreement with the County Council for public access to the towpath, which at that time was not an official right of way. Volunteer labour to help with improvements was again offered by some interested organisations. It is to be hoped that the canal will once again become an asset to the city. British Waterways were busy in late 1975 and again in early 1977 dredging this section of canal in various places on London Road and along Castle Boulevard Nottingham. It could be they were getting their work done in the canal before any work to improve the towpath was carried out.

In another issue of the *Nottingham Weekly Post*, No.316 for 27 May 1976, it was recounted that fourth-year pupils at Fernwood Junior School, Arleston Drive, Wollaton, decided to make a nature trail of the old, dried-up canal bed in the area of Wollaton from Lambourne Drive up to the old Wollaton Colliery site at the end of Bridge Road, Wollaton. Parties of children aged ten to eleven studied the canal bed and towpath over the winter months of 1975 and early 1976. The result of their research was a towpath nature trail. Neighbouring schools were then invited to follow this trail, which, surprisingly, follows a rural route. The children look for and make notes of unusual things such as the ash tree which has taken root in the canal wall between large heavy canal walling stones, lifting them as it grows. In the derelict locks they make notes of the different kinds of moss growing on the walls and on the towpath, noting all the different kinds of wild flowers. It is a marvellous idea; both children and teachers can take credit for creating interest in a lost canal.

Also reported in *Nottingham Weekly Post*, No.322 dated 8 July 1976, was that Broxtowe Council Land Committee was about to complete negotiations for the 5-mile section of canal mentioned earlier, at a cost of £7,350. The Council Recreation and Amenities Department hoped to create a nature trail along the towpath. It·also reported that help had been offered by local Amenity Groups, with working parties to start at a later date.

Since its inauguration, Nottingham Canal Society had put forward objections to Nottingham City Council with regard to its intention to develop the section of canal in Wollaton for housing. The society suggested instead that the site be cleaned up and developed into an industrial museum by restoring the derelict lock chambers, exhibiting narrow boats and Trent barges, the rebuilt locks to be used to demonstrate to people how they work. It was also hoped to keep the towpath as a nature trail. The Nottingham City Council rejected these proposals and carried on with its plans to develop the site for housing, although it did state

Coventry Lane Bridge in 1920;
it is a very different scene today.

that it would like to keep some of the canal features and blend them in with new proposed surroundings. Sadly, the proposed housing development went ahead with no canal features retained except for a small section on the flight of locks. The lock chambers, however, have been levelled.

The society at that time was also hoping to prevent the canal being piped under the proposed new Awsworth Bypass, which was scheduled for building in 1980. Obviously they wanted to see the bypass taken over the canal, just in case restoration to full navigation is achieved at a much later date. The Leisure Services Committee agreed with the Nottingham Canal Society that the Nottingham County Council should be requested to include the Nottingham Canal in its future reclamation programme, and that it would also like to see the Awsworth Bypass, when built, give full navigable headroom over the canal. The bypass held the key to how far the canal could be made navigable, because if headroom was not given, then much of the canal would be lost to eventual navigation. It was a big setback to restoration that when the bypass went ahead it did not give the required headroom due to cost. At a Nottingham Canal Society meeting on

5 February 1979, it was agreed to send a strong letter to all council members about the society's feelings on the matter.

In their preliminary report the society did, of course, make the point that a reconnection with the Erewash Canal would have to be made at a point just below the end of the canal by the new Eastwood Bypass junction, which cuts the canal off from the Great Northern Basin at Langley Mill. The Erewash Canal Preservation & Development Association who attended the inaugural meeting of the society were giving full support. At this point close to the Great Northern Basin on the Nottingham Canal there is only one lock higher than the Erewash Canal; both canals come close together a short distance away from the Erewash Canal's top lock; it wouldn't have been too difficult to reconnect both waterways here. Unfortunately, this did not happen even though the society had a

Horse-drawn narrow boat at Trowell, exact location and date unknown, but it was probably earlier than 1920. The high ground on the left could be Stapleford Hill with the railway line running below. (Nottingham County Library Local History Department)

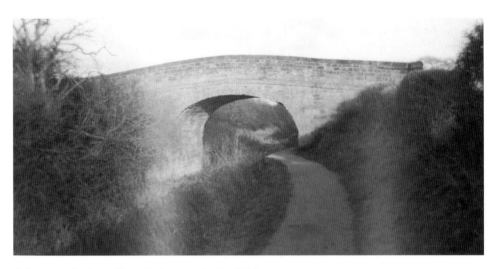

A fine stone bridge at Trowell, photographed in 1996.

feasibility study done. The Inland Waterways Association (East Midlands Region) and the Erewash Canal Preservation & Development Association were asked by the District Council for their observations on the Nottingham Canal Society proposals in view of their past experience and the problems in such a project.

Nottingham Canal Society was able to start working parties once agreement was reach with Broxtowe District Council. The first working party was on Sunday 17 April 1977. Varied work was carried out over the next few months including hedge trimming, bridge building, repairs on the canal bank and general tidying up. It was hard work, for the society membership still only numbered twenty-four. My wife and myself were two of them and I was also a committee member. At working parties, people did attend from other interested groups to boost the numbers.

The first accounts of the Nottingham Canal Society were published on 31 August 1977 and were as follows:

Nottingham Canal Society
Income & Expenditure Account for the year ended 31 August 1977

INCOME

Sponsored Bowhaul	£81 55p
Subscriptions	£46 50p
Donations	£15 10p
Use of Chain Saw	£3
Income from Book Sales (net)	£1 22p
Deposit Account Interest	£0 65p
£148 02p	

EXPENDITURE

Building Materials etc.	£51 85p
Display Stands	£18 66p
Postage, Printing & Stationery	£10 60p
Room Hire for Meetings	£8
Repairs to Borrowed Plant	£2 16p
I.W.A. Subscription	£4
Bank Charges	58p
£95.85	

Surplus of Income over Expenditure for year	£52 17p
Represented by:	
Cash in Bank: Current Account	£23 39p
Deposit Account	£25 65
Cash in Hand	85p
Stock of Books for resale at cost	£2 28p

Swansea Bridge at Trowell in 1921. Could it be that whoever owned the punt tied up opposite the towpath was camping in the field?

Swansea Bridge in 1976. It was boarded up across the towpath to keep people away from land owned by Nottingham County Nurseries. The stop gates are still in place.

Auditors' Report

I have audited the above account from the records, Vouchers presented to me and I certify that they are in agreement therewith.

P. Thorpe

Chartered Accountant

It can be seen from the accounts that the society's income and expenditure were very modest.

The society produced two reports for work to be done along the line of canal from where the canal is cut across by the M1, Trowell to the Kimberlay–Eastwood Bypass embankment at Langley Mill. These reports, known as Scheme A and B, were as follows:

SCHEME A

This involves the restoration of the existing stretch of canal between New Manleys Lane and the enforced terminus at Kimberlay-Eastwood By-pass embankment Langley Mill.

WORK TO BE UNDERTAKEN.

Past work parties have already made a start on this stretch by rebuilding the parapets of Tinsley Road Bridge and excavating some of the infill from beneath the bridge.

A levels survey has shown that the towpath needs raising in the area of the culvert under New Manleys Road Bridge, physical inspection shows that minor repairs to the walling will also be necessary, particularly between Bailey Grove Bridge and the terminus. A small amount of hedge cutting will also need to be carried out to create a continuous footpath from Langley Mill to New Manleys Lane.

The canal down the side of Castle Boulevard, left opposite the towpath. Nottingham Castle can be seen in the distance left of centre. This was taken in 1921.

Quite extensive infill removal will need to be undertaken between Tinsley Road and Bailey Grove Bridge and dredging may also need to be undertaken on the remainder of the canal. The off bank in the region of the old council tip needs strengthening, some of the infill removed will serve this purpose.

The wooden swing bridge between Tinsley Road and New Manleys Road needs to be restored, some timbers need replacing and the ball bearings may need to be replaced.

An overflow weir should be constructed in the region of the tip, on the off bank, at the point where the bank has been breached to facilitate the initial draining of the canal.

Because of the years of neglect in a waterless state it is certain that there will be a few leaks on the embankments, an accepted method of dealing with these is to dig a trench up to six feet deep in the towpath, approximately six inches wide and re-puddle the trench with clay. In this respect particular attention should be paid to the section of embankment at either side of Bailey Grove Bridge where there are cottages at the foot of the bank, which could be affected by damp in the event of a leak in the vicinity.

Water supply

There is at present no feed to this section of canal, any water present being land drainage water. However the surface water drained off the Kimberley-Eastwood by-pass has been culverted under the canal near Bailey Grove Bridge and at present discharges into the Erewash Canal, it is suggested that this could be diverted into the Nottingham Canal to provide some water to at least keep the puddle from drying out.

A steady, permanent feed can only be supplied at such time as the channel is re-dug back to the original Giltbrook feeder.

Timings

It is difficult to judge the timings for voluntary works as it depends to a large extent on the numbers turning out, however it is envisaged that the above works would take a minimum of two years.

It is possible that a Job Creation Scheme could be run on the canal, this would of course reduce the length of time taken for completion.

Costs

These costs have been estimated and are for guidance only; they do not include any labour costs, which should be zero as the work is to be carried out by volunteers.

Swing bridge restoration	£500
Bank raising and walling	£500
Infill removal	£1000.00
Machine maintenance and tools	£400
TOTAL	£2,400

SCHEME B

This scheme involves the re-watering of the section of canal between the M1 and Coronation Road aqueduct.

WORK TO BE UNDERTAKEN

The only feed to this section of canal comes from a stream which feeds down the Robbinetts Arm near Cossall and of course land drainage. At present all water coming down the Arm is being lost through one or more leaks in the canal bed, a major one at the overflow weir approximately 200 yards up the Arm. It is suggested this weir be either fully repaired or a

Above: Robbinetts swing bridge in 1963; this bridge has now been replaced with a road and the arm culverted under. (Peter Stevenson)

Left: Robbinetts Arm overflow weir; when this picture was taken in 1921 the arm was badly silted up.

Above: Weed cleaning by members of The British Trust for Conservation Volunteers at Cossall in 1996. (Broxtowe Borough Council)

Below: The section of canal at the side of Cossall Road; the footbridge over the canal centre gives access from the road to the canal towpath.

Above: Members of The British Trust for Conservation Volunteers at work cleaning out the canal at Cossall in 1996. (Broxtowe Borough Council)

Below: The Junction of Robbinetts Arm and Main Line at Cossall, photographed in 1996.

new one constructed on the canal side of the culverted bridge over the Arm and the old one sealed up. A portion of the width of the Arm could then be dredge to provide a good channel down which water could easily flow into the canal.

When a feed is assured to the canal lengths of the channel can then be isolated in turn and allowed to fill to a predetermined level, this can be effected by the use of stop planks and/or stop gates along the canal or by inserting temporary sheet steel stank across the canal.

In this way a length of canal which includes the feeder would be isolated and when the water level reaches the desired height excess water will weir over the stank into other parts of the canal. The section in water can then be tested for leaks along the banks and necessary action taken before proceeding to fully water the next section.

At the same time as dredging is taking place on the Arm it would be timely to construct a launching ramp into the canal for the future use of trailer boats, a suitable site would be in the region of the junction of the main line and the Robbinetts Arm.

There is a swing bridge on this section which needs restoring, Trowell Parish Council have requested that a footbridge be constructed across the canal possibly on the site of a swing bridge between the Robbinetts Arm and Trowell, in view of the possible use by boats on the canal within a small number of years any provision of a new bridge should take this into account.

When the length in question is permanently re-watered dredging should be carried out along most of the canal to remove the majority of the weed beds in the navigation channel, this will not only provide for the easy passage of boats but will be of value to wild fowl and aquatic life by helping to reduce the deoxygenating in the water.

In the area of the slipway parking and picnicking facilities could be set up to cater for persons using the canal for their recreation.

TIMINGS

Work could start on the Arm early in the New Year providing that British Waterways Board approval is forthcoming as they are the present owners.

Work on the main line of the canal cannot really start until such time as water feed is assured to the canal.

Work on the bridges could be undertaken before the water feed is assured.

COSTS

These costs have been estimated and are for guidance only; they do not include any labour costs, which should be zero as the work is to be carried out by volunteers.

Overgrown canal bed at Trowell between Trowell Nurseries and the M1 in 1979.

Stop planks, stop gates and stanks	£900
Slipway	£400
Puddling	£1,000
Overflow weir	£250
Swing bridge (restore)	£500
Swing bridge (new)	£1,200
Total	£4,200

In 1978 a breach occurred in the canal at Trowell on the embankment carrying the canal up to the M1. It was not disastrous but could have slowly become worse if it had been left. The Nottingham Canal Society undertook to do this work after they were approached by Broxtowe Borough Council to help repair the breach. Work was carried out by the society, helped by prison labour from one of the local prisons. East Midlands Waterway Recovery Group supplied the machinery for the work. The work was done by, firstly, sealing off the canal above the breach, pumping out the water and clearing out the canal bed. This was then covered with loose gravel. Pipes were purchased from Stanton Ironworks, Derbyshire, which were then laid on top of the gravel from the culvert under the M1 past the breach to where the canal was first sealed off. A hired crane was to lay the pipes on the canal bed. A concrete base was then built across the canal at the place where it was sealed off. The canal walling stones from the area of the breach were removed and rebuilt across this concrete base up to the height of the towpath, except for the entrance to the pipes, where an overflow was built to take water into the newly laid pipes.

In February the same year it was also decided to step up the campaign to have the Awsworth Bypass built giving head room for navigation and not to culvert the canal – it was known that if this were to happen all hope of full navigation from Trowell to Langley Mill would be lost. Nottinghamshire County Council had refused to build a bridge over the canal, stating it would cost £428,000. Whilet the society agreed Awsworth needed a bypass to ease traffic flow, it still believed the canal to be worth saving. It wrote letters to all Broxtowe councillors with a plea to save the canal. At that time the canal was in Broxtowe Council's plans for restoration, which put the society in conflict with the County Council.

Other groups were also interested in the canal; these enthusiasts felt that a more feasible proposition would be to terminate the canal alongside the M1 at Trowell. The site here, at their suggested terminus, could be developed into an attractive Marina Complex. This, of course, was contrary to the suggestions of the Nottingham Canal Society. This could have been a good idea and would have avoided the costly expense of taking the canal under the M1. It would have meant the loss of a 2-mile section the other side of the motorway up to Coventry Lane, Trowell. These 2 miles could be made use of for other amenities. It was the view of these groups that the structure, which carries the pipes over the road at Awsworth, could be modified so as to carry the water in a trough, which would allow boats of 6ft 10in beams to pass through should the canal be restored.*

Nottingham Canal Society held its first AGM at the Gate Inn, Awsworth, on 4 October 1977. Only twelve of the present membership attended. It was hoped that this attendance would improve when members and the public saw what could be achieved, and what had been achieved during the previous twelve months. With a small society there are often more sleeping members than active. It was pointed out that since the society started some work had been done with working parties at least once a month, with two parties in some months when possible. Permission had now been granted for the society to carry out work on the derelict flight of locks from Woodyard Lane, Wollaton, to the site of Lock No.17. The work mainly consisted of keeping the area clean and tidy, cutting hedges and removing accumulated rubbish. It was hoped, once people could see the area was being cleaned up, it might stop the indiscriminate dumping. People still regularly used the towpath for walking. Nottingham City Council were not willing to put forward any money towards the cost, so any expense which might arise from work carried out would have to be paid for by the society. The society was a registered charity doing what it could to raise funds; waste paper was being

*Information from a report in the *Beeston Gazette & Echo* dated 23 December 1976.

Old winding hole at Trowell, east of the M1, in 1979.

The section of canal between Nottingham Road (A609) at Trowell, looking east in 1979. What appears to be a bridge in the centre is the M1, which cuts the canal here.

Above: Breach in canal bank at Trowell in 1978. Nottingham Canal Society carried out repairs.

Left: A view of the breach at Trowell from the field below the canal, taken in 1978.

collected but in the early days only in small amounts, owing to the difficulty of storage. It had once been hoped to lease Jackmans Farm, Eastwood. The farm was owned by the National Coal Board and was close to the canal, but it had been badly damaged by vandals, making it an unsafe place to store paper.

Funds had received a boost, with a £200 donation from Shell UK Ltd in conjunction with their 'Shell Inland Waterways Restoration Awards'. £150 of this was given towards the rebuilding of the swing bridge at Bailey Grove, Eastwood. Broxtowe Council gave £100 to help with rebuilding Tinsley Road Bridge, also in the Eastwood area. The hard work put in so far had all been worthwhile considering the small membership the society had, and members put in great efforts and found time to bow haul a 70ft narrow boat from Halesowen, Birmingham to Nottingham, to raise funds and get publicity for the society. A sponsored walk had also been organised.

It was pointed out to members that while some work could be done by volunteers, other work would require experienced people as it would be beyond the scope of volunteers. Contractors would have to be used sometimes. Supervised work would consist of channel dredging, bridge building, lock construction, and overflow weir construction and rubbish removal. Work put out to contractors would probably entail lift bridges and fixed bridge construction, and extensive channel excavation. Enquiries were made into the cost of providing factory-made culverts for the reconstruction of fixed bridges; these could considerably reduce the cost. The cost of a 10m length of culvert giving navigable headroom

Trowell Bridge, looking west in 1921 on a calm day, showing an excellent reflection of the cottage, which is still there.

was approximately £3,500. The cost of re-excavating 1 mile of canal channel to navigable standards would be approximately £1,600.

The most important item after work on restoration was complete would be reconnection to the navigable waterways system via the Erewash Canal. The Erewash Canal Preservation & Development Association had agreed to offset the cost of building the new lock required to connect the two waterways. They had decided to concentrate their efforts more with the Nottingham Canal Society since the scheme they had hoped to be involved with on the Cromford Canal had fallen through. Labour to carry out this work would involve Nottingham and Erewash groups, plus the Inland Waterways Association and East Midlands Waterways Recovery Group. The Erewash Canal Preservation & Development Association were to provide figures on sizes of boats passing through their waterway; figures provided showed that 90 per cent of boats using their canal were of the narrow boat type with a beam of 6ft 10in. Nevertheless, this was expected to be many years away. The Nottingham Canal Society produced a small magazine every three months, which was sent out to members, giving details of working parties and keeping members up to date with developments regarding the canal. This magazine was named *Top Cut* and only thirteen were printed, the last one in March 1979. In the last magazine, in the chairman's notes it was stated it would cost £428,000 to build a culvert allowing headroom under the planned Awsworth Bypass. Neither Nottinghamshire County Council or Broxtowe Borough Council could afford that kind of money.

> In view of what is an uncertain future for the canal the committee have to decide on the future of the society. We would like to hear from members, as to what you as members feel should happen to the society. With regard to working parties we have pledged to Broxtowe Borough Council that we will complete work at Trowell and on the swing bridge at Eastwood, but after that the present members of working parties will not undertake any more work.

Since no further developments regarding full restoration took place, the society was closed down shortly afterwards.

On 23 April 1981, Awsworth Parish Council rejected a Broxtowe Borough Council plan for the restoration of the canal from Park Hill to Newtons Lane. Broxtowe Borough Council planned to set trees along the line of the canal and landscape the area between Newtons Lane and the Bennerley Viaduct; this viaduct was the subject of discussions over how it might be saved. It was a surprise to Broxtowe Borough Council that this view should be taken by Awsworth Parish Council as this area was used for many years for fishing by a local angling club and is the best part of the upper canal left, plus the fact that the National Coal Board were supposed to put the canal back to how it was after carrying out open-cast coal mining, this arrangement having been agreed by them.

A twenty-eight-page report on the canal's potential was adopted by Broxtowe Borough Council by just one vote in October 1982. Also in the report was the recommendation that a £103,000 plan to supply water to the canal over the next three years should be investigated in more detail. It was hoped to obtain a temporary water supply from the Erewash Canal; no mention was made, however, of how this was to be done. The canal was to be filled in section by section in some areas, to aid the repair of leaks. The final phase of the three-year plan would include pedestrian improvements, signposting and landscaping. The councillors were urged to support the 'courageous beginning' towards restoration, which was a positive step against what at the time seemed an increasing trend to destroy derelict waterways.

The long-awaited towpath from Beeston to Nottingham was finally opened at an official ceremony on 9 June 1982, six years after plans had been approved by Nottinghamshire Leisure Services Committee. Mr Illtyd Harrington of British Waterways was there to cut the ribbon. The Lord Mayor of Nottingham, Mr Peter Burgess, was also in attendance. Mr Harrington said, 'The project had been imaginative and a thoughtful one for the people of Nottingham and it is up to the young to take an interest in it.' The mayor said, 'He was delighted to be involved in the ceremony.'

In July 1984, conservation volunteers started work on a restoration project on the canal at Cossall. Councillor John Finch, chairman of the Nottingham Canal sub-committee, said that due to the efforts of the British Trust for Conservation Volunteers restoration of the canal had been speeded up. The help would be appreciated with the Nottingham Canal Society having folded a few years earlier, once it was realised the canal was never going to be restored to a navigable standard. As it was only a small society, support fell away, which was a great disappointment after all the early efforts. These volunteers give up their free time and holidays to carry out work, and some of these volunteers came from America and Holland. The work started with a two-day trial, so that when work started in earnest they would be using the right tools and techniques. Working thigh-deep in mud they were taking plants out by hand, removing predominant types of plants from the canal bed to enable less common species to flourish. Broxtowe Borough Council provided a shelter near the canal for breaks. It was hoped the volunteers would return again next year. The Territorial Army had also offered help on the construction of a new bridge, with work to start in October. The volunteers would also be working on a 200m section of the Robbinetts Arm of the canal, this being the only remaining water supply into the canal. Because of its neglected condition, the canal can only be properly assessed after a certain amount of work had been completed; for this reason the council had advocated a cautious approach. This was where the advantage of volunteer labour could be two-fold: their work could also be selective by providing a feed back of information that could have been helpful at a later date. The council was allocating funds on an annual basis for work on the canal. The budget for 1984–85 was £22,500. In August the same year an attractive folder, to contain progress reports on restoring sections of the canal, was produced by the council, in the hope it would act as a stimulus to interested groups using the canal for recreation and outdoor activities. With restoration starting in earnest one of the first tasks would be to stop water loss from principal sources of supply.

There were problems with the canal embankment during 1985 when water started leaking through it at Trowell, causing concern to residents living close by. Restoration work was halted for fear of a bank slippage. Broxtowe Borough Council sub-committee, supervising the restoration, asked for £6,000 to investigate the strength of the embankment. Planning permission was being sought to infill this section of canal with waste material but this also caused concern because to fill the canal with inert material could put additional loads on the embankment which could be critical to its safety. These fears were raised after an earlier embankment failure at Cossall. It was felt that failure of a soil embankment would be less catastrophic than one containing even a small amount of water. Conservation groups objected to the loss of wetland habitat should the canal be filled in. Later the same year the council withdrew the application to infill sections of the canal, so with restoration work halted for the time being, it was decided to take the opportunity to assess the soundness of the whole canal from Trowell to Awsworth.

Later the same year the all-clear was given for the £6,000 survey to go ahead to test the stability of some sections of the canal, which were causing concern. To analyse the embankment, boreholes would be drilled at points along the towpath, samples to be studied at Trent Polytechnic. The areas giving most concern were at the back of Ilkeston Road, Trowell, The Highway at Dead Lane, Cossall, and Coronation Road, Cossall. This survey must have found these areas to be leaking and unstable, because Broxtowe Borough Council held a meeting on 15 September 1986, again to discuss plans over whether to infill the canal in areas around Trowell and Cossall. It was expected that the cost of infill could be expensive and would involve a 1,600m section from Nottingham Road, Trowell, to the lay-by on Cossall Road. When filled in, it would ease concerns of local residents. Attending the meeting to voice proposals against this action were the Nature Conservancy Council, the County Trust for Nature Conservation and Nottingham History Department. After a study carried out of over 150 species of plants and a diverse list of insects in the area, the case put forward was regarding the decline of wetlands in the county over the last ten years. Man-made wetlands were becoming increasingly important.

The cost of work on the canal was still rumbling on in April 1987. Then Broxtowe Borough Council estimated it could cost up to £160,000 to infill the section of canal in the Trowell area, which amounted to over 1p on the borough rate. The sub-committee, who wanted to use £58,200 from contingency funds, had agreed plans. It was understood the council would have to borrow the money; department charges would amount to £10,300 a year for the next ten years. The latest hiccups in a series of setbacks were causing controversy: firstly the re-introduction of water in some areas caused the embankment to slip. A revised scheme was abandoned after councillors were told it would cost £300,000. Other ideas were also dropped due to the cost and some councillors where questioning why it was costing the council £29,700 to infill the canal when it was to be used for tipping – it should be making a profit from tipping.

The canal cleaned out at Trowell Bridge by Broxtowe Borough Council, ready for lining in 1995; note how good the canal wall is after 200 years! (Broxtowe Borough Council)

Taken six days later, when the lining had been put down. (Broxtowe Borough Council)

In 1997 when this picture was taken at Trowell, nature had started to take over the area again. The lining, laid two years earlier, appears to be coming to the top in places probably due to air underneath.

Infilling taking place at Trowell, to the west of the bridge in 1989. The towpath is on the right. The work was again carried out by Broxtowe Borough Council. (Broxtowe Borough Council)

It was expected there would be a total cost of £37,238 for draining the section of canal from Nottingham Road to Cossall lay-by. Included in this price was the creation of a footpath and bridleway, landscaped pond areas and the supply of topsoil. The council expected to offset against this £7,538 for tipping rights, with a £2,600 grant from the Countryside Commission. Off-site drainage work could cost £24,445. When work was completed it would transform a derelict canal into an excellent recreation area. The policy committee approved the allocation of the £58,200 from contingency funds. Work was expected to start on 1 May.

Some councillors were still not very happy with the situation, saying, 'The council has inherited a problem which could be best described as a derelict stinking eyesore'. It is fortunate that these councillors were in the minority because the canal in the area is now a very pleasant place.

In May 1987 officials from Broxtowe Borough Council and members from the Awsworth Angling Club restocked the restored section of canal from Newtons Lane to Park Hill, Awsworth, with 600 fish – a mixture of carp, roach and bream. These fish had been transported by road from Humberside. By the time the angling season started on 16 June, a further 600 fish had been added. A few years ago the canal had been wiped out by open-cast mining and it was not clear whether it would be reconstituted by the Coal Board; it eventually was, at their cost.

Footbridge over the canal at Mill Lane, Cossall, after clearance work by The British Trust for Conservation Volunteers in 1996.

Above: Cossall Colliery Drift passing over the canal in 1957. (Peter Stevenson)

Below: Canal embankment at Awsworth in 1921, before it was piped across Coronation Road in 1958.

In October 1994, almost 200 years to the day since the investors met to promote the construction of a canal from the river Trent in Nottingham to Langley Mill, a celebration by conservationists took place at Cossall to mark the anniversary. Most of the work taken on by Broxtowe Borough Council over the years, since the purchase of the section of canal they now own, had by then been completed. The deputy mayor, Councillor John Booth, attended the celebration and cut a tape at the start of a towpath tour and issued badges to the first patrol of Cossall Wildlife Watch, a volunteer group who safeguarded habitats and explained interesting points to visitors. The canal now offered tremendous scope in its new role as a nature reserve. Mr Ken Wood, senior wildlife warden, recorded his appreciation of the support given to the project over the years by the Borough Council, the British Trust for Conservation Volunteers and Nottinghamshire Wildlife Trust.

Another group, The Robbinetts Action Group, an anti-open-cast pressure group, had cause for celebration when it was confirmed that British Coal had excluded the Robbinetts Arm from its plans to outcrop 500 acres between Cossall and Trowell. Earlier the same year, British Coal offered to buy this section of land from Broxtowe Borough Council but they refused to sell.

Further up the canal at the Langley Mill end, in 1985 the Shell Awards to Waterways contributed £1,000 to help rebuild the swing bridge over the entrance to the Nottingham Canal, in front of where the stop lock was once situated. The Cromford Canal is slowly being extended away from the Great Northern Basin; to help this section of canal with the water supply, the feeder from Moorgreen Reservoir, which was built by the Nottingham Canal Co., was re-opened in the 1990s after considerable dredging had been carried out. This is the only natural water supply to this section of the Cromford Canal.

Two buses passing each other on the newly widened road under the canal at Awsworth, shortly after opening in 1958, now Coronation Road. (Peter Stevenson)

Entrance to pipes across Coronation Road, Awsworth, in 1977. The pipes were put in to maintain a water supply when the road was widened from a single carriageway to a double in 1958.

Concrete pipe structure over Coronation Road, Awsworth, in 1977; they no longer carry water, the level having dropped so low.

A small isolated section of canal between Coronation Road and Shilo Way, Awsworth; it was along this section that a wharf connected with the Babbington Branch Railway.

Work taking place at Cossall Marsh under the direction of Broxtowe Borough Council, in 1989. (Broxtowe Borough Council)

Above: Broxtowe Borough Council working on the canal at Cossall Marsh; the car scrap yard is in the background here in 1989. (Broxtowe Borough Council)

Left: Remains of a narrow boat rotting at the old brickworks wharf near to Newtons Lane in 1977; both boat and wharf have now gone.

Dredging at Newtons Lane in 1987/88, once again carried out by Broxtowe Borough Council. (Broxtowe Borough Council)

The canal at Newtons Lane a year later after re-watering the towpath on the left, in 1989. (Broxtowe Borough Council)

Cleaning out the canal bed at Cossall under the direction of Broxtowe Borough Council in 1995. (Broxtowe Borough Council)

Above: The section of canal at Awsworth used by Cotmanhay Angling Club between Newtons Lane and Park Hill at Newtons Lane end in 1996.

Opposite below: A working party cleaning out the canal at Cossall, close to the junction with Robbinetts Arm, in 1996. The overgrown towpath is on the right.

Further along the same section of canal at Park Hill end in 1996.

7

MEADOW LANE TO LENTON CHAIN

Starting from the bottom of the canal and working upward in the direction of Langley Mill, Trent Lock No.1 is the first on Nottingham Canal. It connects the canal to the river Trent just below Trent Bridge, opposite Nottingham Forest football ground. The football ground came a long time after both Nottingham and Grantham canals, the entrance to Grantham Canal being just below the football ground. The entrance lock into the Grantham Canal is in working order after restoration by the Grantham Canal Restoration Society some years ago. It does, however, only lead to a small section of canal, the canal having been cut by road improvements. It was here many years ago that there was a wooden horse bridge spanning the river between both canals; it was washed away in a bad flood and never replaced. The river is very wide at this point. Getting a horse across pulling a narrow boat would not have been a easy task for the boatman.

Trent Lock No.1 is in very good condition and well kept. Close by is a water point, rubbish disposal area and toilets are also available. There is a chemical toilet disposal, kept clean and tidy. There is a footbridge over the lock just above the bottom gates. It needs careful manoeuvring to enter the lock from the river, which is fast moving; pontoons have been added in recent years to help boats when waiting. The lock house is close to the lock with a neat garden bordering the side of the lock opposite the towpath. To operate this lock does not require a windlass to work the paddle gear, as handles are fitted to the gearing. (A windlass is a large key with a handle which fits over the spindle attached to the gearing to wind the paddles up or down to fill and empty the lock chamber.) It is not a widely used method to have handles permanently fitted to lock paddle gears because unauthorised use can cause severe loss of water or damage.

Above the lock on the towpath side is an iron fence up to the water's edge, with a gate; this is locked and can only be opened with a British Waterways key. It is not possible to get access to this section of towpath, which is approximately 100m, unless in a boat or in possession of a British Waterways key. Facilities are provided for boaters above the lock. British Waterways have good reason for keeping the area secure.

Trent Street, Nottingham. The train crossing is on the Great Northern Railway Viaduct. This viaduct was demolished some years ago. This was taken in 1921.

On leaving Trent Lock No.1 in the direction of Nottingham City centre the canal turns to the right. The towpath here was newly laid in 2004 with block stones and fitted with mooring rings. On the left opposite the towpath there was once an old warehouse which was used by British Waterways. At the beginning of this right turn a footbridge passes over the canal which joined two factories on either side of the canal. Both factories were demolished a few years ago and replaced with two very pleasant housing developments on both sides of the canal. The footbridge has been retained and improved. The outer building on London Road, part of the factory complex, has been retained and turned into flats; it was originally a tannery and was owned by Turney Brothers for years. The flats have been named Turney's Court. The first bridge over the canal is Meadow Lane Road Bridge, built in 1907 over 100 years after the canal. It is followed very closely by Bridge No.1, a fine bridge built from masonry stone and in excellent condition. On the side of this bridge can be found an old barrel-shaped bridge protector used when boats were horse drawn to stop ropes cutting into the sides of the bridge. This bridge protector is the only one of its type I've ever seen. When first made, it would have rotated when a rope passed over it; grooves can be seen in it made by ropes many years ago. Bollards are across the approaches to this bridge on both sides so that it no longer carries traffic, but it is still used by pedestrians. Access to the towpath can be gained from Meadow Lane.

After Bridge No.1 the canal runs straight along the side of London Road; the road is much higher than the canal with a wall all along the side so nothing can be seen from canal level except tree tops and the odd tall building on the other side of the road. The towpath is very good, being block paved all the way into

Fellows Morton & Clayton Warehouse once housed the Canal Museum; there are now new restaurants on both sides that can be very busy at lunchtimes. This picture was taken in 2004.

The canal in Nottingham in 1921; Carrington Street Bridge is in the centre with a tram crossing. Fellows Morton & Clayton Warehouse is on the left, just past the boat. The bridge on the right with the towpath over it was built by Midland Counties Railway Co. in 1839 to serve their warehouse and goods yard.

Taken in 1976 a little further along the canal than No.17, the bridge to the warehouse is still there but no longer in use. The large building on the left was once owned by the Trent Navigation Co. and later used by British Waterways.

Nottingham before the next bridge, County Road (added many years after the canal's construction); along the towpath side there is a small grass bank with a fence, beyond which are business premises, Mower World with a small factory business in between. Just here, there used to be a small dock with a towpath bridge over its entrance. This dock would have accommodated probably three or four boats and was known as Sanitary Wharf. It was used for some years for shipping excrement by canal from earth closets of Nottingham tenement houses. (The excrement was a valuable commodity and, when treated, was sold to farmers along both Nottingham & Grantham canals.) The businesses which back onto the canal here have their fronts on Iremonger Road, named after Albert Iremonger who played in goal for Notts County Football Club, the oldest professional football club in the United Kingdom, founded in 1862. Albert stood 6ft 5½ins tall; he played for County for a number of years after the First World War into the early 1920s. County football ground is close by here, having entrances on Iremonger Road, County Road and Meadow Lane, from which the ground takes its name.

Once through County Road Bridge, which is a wide single span, on the opposite side to the towpath can be found the stone base from a cast-iron gentlemen's urinal which was there for many years before being taken away to the Industrial Museum in Wollaton Park, Nottingham. There are more small factories on the towpath side and London Road is on the left. All along this section the towpath is paved, making it easy to walk. Some of the factories are hidden from view behind large advertising hoardings. Under the next bridge is a flood marker

Taken from Fellows Morton & Clayton Wharf in 1989, Midland Counties Railway Co.'s warehouse, once behind the bridge, had been demolished to make way for a new Magistrates' Court.

showing the height of the 1952 flood; there have been higher floods in 1875 and 1947. Many years ago, before it was lifted much higher than the canal, London Road was known as Flood Road because the river Trent, flooding frequently, inundated the area. The next bridge is the first railway bridge to cross the canal and carries the main line into Nottingham Midland Station; it is a wrought-iron girder bridge of two spans built by Midland Counties Railway around 1850. The wider of the two spans is over the canal and is 9ft 6in (2.895m) high with a span of 34ft 9in (10.598m); the second span is 10ft (3.050m) high with a span of 18ft (5.490m). There is a slight change: London Road is still with the canal but now gets even higher, built on concrete piers over the railway which has just passed over the canal. It comes down again on more concrete piers to its original level. More factories are on the towpath side.

The next bridge was a change-over bridge, which took the canal towpath from right side to left. It was a fine stone structure, which had survived nearly 190 years and still had its number 2 plates in the wall. Once again, road improvements in the 1980s have changed things, as now this new bridge is a two-way road bridge. It is still possible to walk from one side of the canal to the other over the new bridge by crossing the bridge on the pavement. On both sides of this new bridge, the leads up to it from canal towpath level – taken by horses in the days of horse-drawn traffic – have been retained, and this is also a good place to access the towpath. This was the only change-over bridge on the canal; from here the towpath remained on the left up to Langley Mill; up to this point the distance covered is approximately three quarters of a mile. There is a good restaurant here called Hooters, high above the canal close to what was once abutments where the Great Northern Railway entered Nottingham. The viaduct that carried the railway over the canal here was taken down in 1997.

Here the canal widens out (this wide area is the last place to wind a 70ft narrow boat before the river), the main line turning sharply to the left. London Road, which has been with the canal all along this stretch opposite the towpath, now passes over the canal on this bend. What was left of the Poplar Arm to Sneinton turned off to the right with a towpath down the right side from Bridge No.2. This branch has now been filled in. This took place at the same time the railway viaduct was dismantled in 1977. The Poplar Branch had become very silted up in recent years, making the area dismal. There was a corrugated-iron bridge across this branch a short distance from the junction, joining factories on both sides. The bridge had a keystone dated 1862 and inscribed 'River Lean Culvert' with the name 'Richard Birkin Mayor'. Richard Birkin was mayor at the time; it was one of his duties to lay the keystone and officially open the bridge. The Great Northern Railway came down the side of the Poplar Branch where it had a small station and goods yard at Sneinton. It passed over the canal at the junction, continuing down the side of the canal towpath on a viaduct, turning right and passing over the canal heading north into Nottingham. A new Premier Lodge Hotel overlooks the junction, which is now a large winding hole. On the bend facing this hotel on the towpath can be found an old, well-worn wooden bollard.

Once under London Road the canal is straight for about 200m. Some old canalside buildings are still close to the canal opposite the towpath in between the canal and Canal Street. The towpath is all paved here and easy to walk. It was along here the Great Northern Railway Viaduct followed the canal for approximately 400m, passing over it just after it turned slightly left, shortly before reaching Trent Street where it joined another Great Northern Line from Loughborough, Leicestershire, where they carried on to Nottingham Victoria Station. Only the clock tower remains from the station today. It is now a very large shopping centre taking the same name of Victoria.

Some of the old canal buildings opposite the towpath are occupied with small industries, one such being a carpet warehouse entrance on Canal Street. There is now no sign of the many wharves that lined the canal here many years ago. Along the towpath there used to be some very old iron railings by the water's edge; they were removed when the towpath was improved. The canal runs straight now for some distance after passing under a new footbridge, which leads to the new building for Capital One; it follows the towpath for a good distance but is set well back. The towpath is very wide at this point and offers a number of seats.

Next is Trent Street Road Bridge, followed closely by yet another railway viaduct that carried the aforementioned line from Loughborough. This railway viaduct, built by Great Northern Railway in railway blue bricks, has a large arch over the canal 24ft 4in (7.411m) high, with a span of 45ft 4in (13.826m) wide. When the canal was built Trent Street Bridge was a wrought-iron footbridge.

New Nottingham Magistrates' Court. The canal bridge that served the warehouse and sidings remains, and has tastefully fitted in to its new surroundings. This was taken in 2000.

Taken from in front of the new Magistrates' Court, the refurbished British Waterways building is in the background here in 2000.

There is good access to the canal with a new pathway at the side of the Capital One building. The viaduct was not used for many years after the railway was dismantled, but is now utilised for the new Nottingham Electric Transit and is the first station on the line at Nottingham end. It was opened on 9 March 2004 with sixteen stops from Nottingham to Hucknall, a town in north Nottinghamshire. There is also a branch line to Hucknall Phoenix.

After the railway viaduct, just a short distance away is Carrington Street Road Bridge. It dates from 1841 and has a very attractive rosette balustrade. The land for building this bridge sold to Nottingham Corporation by Nottingham Canal Co. for £1,772 2s 6d (£1,772 12p). At the side of Carrington Street Bridge, British Waterways have installed a water point. On the opposite side here before Carrington Street is Nottingham County Court. The entrance is on Canal Street.

Once under Carrington Street Bridge, the canal becomes much wider. This area has been greatly improved and is very pleasant. The towpath is wide with good grassy areas and trees. A little way back from the canal is the new Nottingham Magistrates' Court, an attractive building that fits into the surroundings very well. In front of the Magistrates' Court, a canal bridge on the towpath has been retained; no towpath went under this bridge. The bridge was built by Midland Counties Railway Co. in 1839 at a cost of £306 15s (£306 80p). It is 8ft 10in (2.893m) high with a span of 23ft 4in (7.711m). The bridge opened out into a large basin with wharves for unloading goods from boats for the sheds and warehouses of Midland County Railway Co., before it was demolished to build the new Magistrates' Court. The warehouse was a great eight-storey Victorian building, brick built and with loading doors on each floor from which goods could be hoisted up from boats waiting at wharves below.

Next comes another new footbridge over the canal just after the last mentioned towpath bridge. This footbridge leads from the front of Nottingham Magistrates' Court to the new bars and restaurants opposite the towpath. This area is known as Castle Wharf and is a busy place with some character. New buildings have been mixed in among the old. Fellows Morton & Clayton, the well-known canal carriers, had their officers here for many years. For some years it was used by Nottingham City Council for a Waterways Museum, a very good museum with some excellent exhibits. It was opened to the public for the first time on 30 May 1981. It is now a restaurant and still retains the front of the old warehouse showing Fellows Morton & Clayton in the original large white letters. Also close by in an old warehouse is a fish restaurant called Joshers. This whole area is now bustling, with outside tables and chairs from different restaurants along the wharf creating a scene that couldn't be more different to what it would have been 200 years ago.

If visiting by boat, this is an excellent place to moor up to take in the interesting attractions of Nottingham. For anyone who has never visited the city, there are many places to see both old and new, most being only a short distance from the canal. Regarding places with an historical background, first on the list is Nottingham Castle, an interesting place with free admission on most days. The castle has a museum which contains porcelain, Stone Age flint tools, a memorial to Captain Albert Ball VC, a famous pilot of the First World War, with some of his personal documents and other items including a cigarette case with a bullet mark on it, which saved his life. Outside the castle walls on Castle Road is the statue of Robin Hood; a short distance down from here is what is renowned to be the oldest inn in England, The Trip to Jerusalem. Caves beneath reach far out under the castle, used by the inn to store beers. In the same area is Brew House Yard Museum which has a mock-up of a 1940s school classroom. The Old Market Square is well worth a visit to see the Council House with its two large stone lions in front and dome with clock on top, the clock called 'Little John' which is second to Big Ben in London.

Nottingham has two of the largest undercover shopping centres in the British Isles, these being Victoria Centre and Broad Marsh Centre; the latter is nearest the canal side of the city centre and just a five-minute walk from moorings between Carrington Street and Wilford Street bridges. Broad Marsh Centre is the latest addition (from within this shopping centre it is possible to visit Nottingham's caves); Victoria Centre is the largest. The Victoria Centre has a Water Clock inside designed by Emett. Every quarter of an hour the clock plays a tune, while figures around the clock turn. It is a great attraction for both parents and children. If visiting the city it would be worth taking time out to see The Galleries of Justice and Tales of Robin Hood.

On the opposite side to the towpath, at the moorings just mentioned, there occurred a violent explosion at the public wharf on 28 September 1818. It was quite a catastrophe at the time. Twenty-one barrels of gunpowder exploded while being delivered to the company's warehouse. The explosion was so severe it completely destroyed the warehouse and several boats, killing two men. The blast from the explosion was felt in many parts of town. It would seem the whole affair was caused by one man employed in the boat delivering the gunpowder, when he ignited some powder that had leaked from one barrel in the consignment of twenty-one. The insurance company maintained the damage was caused solely by the explosion, refusing to pay on these grounds. The canal company, in an effort to get compensation for their loss, brought an action against the Nottingham Boat Co., which they won. They were awarded £1,000 compensation with half the costs of the action also in their favour. The Nottingham Boat Co., however, were unable to pay, having still only paid half ten years later.

A little further on, opposite the towpath, is what can only be described as a wonderful canalside warehouse some five storeys high with loading doors on all floors, from which hoists would have been used to unload cargo from boats waiting below. It was firstly the headquarters of The Trent Navigation Co., whose name can still be seen in large white letters all along the top. It was then owned for some years by British Waterways. It is now let out in small units. On the ground floor there is a modern gym and a bar, with mainly offices on the upper floors. The transformation of the old warehouse has been done without changing the exterior, just cleaning it up and improving the area. Close to the old

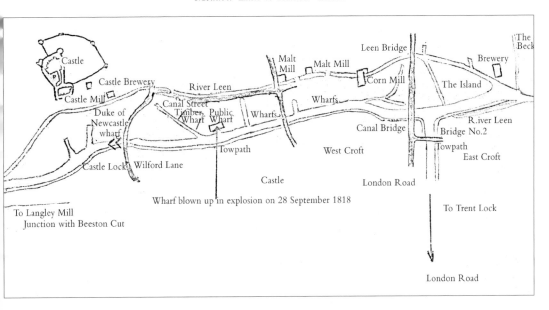

Sketch map for the 1800s showing the public wharf where the explosion took place on 28 September 1818. (Kevin Chell)

warehouse are two new modern buildings, the offices of the *Nottingham Evening Post* and Radio Nottingham.

The next bridge is Wilford Street, of similar design to Carrington Street, again a wrought-iron girder built with a height above the canal of 9ft 5in (2.870m) and a span of 36ft (10.980m). The canal turns slightly to the right before passing under the bridge. Also on the towpath before the bridge are six old and unusual mooring posts, approximately 3ft (1m) tall, 3in in diameter, with a mooring ring at the bottom, recently painted black and white by British Waterways. Directly under the bridge is a very short distance to the bottom gates of Castle Lock. The locks are in fine condition and fairly busy in summer months. The overflow weir round the lock is underground and empties out through the bridge. At the lock side opposite the towpath is the Navigation Inn, built in Victorian times. Another public house was built on the site in 1787, demolished to make way for the Navigation Inn. It was here that passenger boats stopped en route to Cromford and Leicester. Behind the high wall to the left were stables for the canal horses. It is a good place for a meal with chairs and tables outside along the lock side. At the side of the lock on the towpath is an old canal mile post, painted black, so thickly that it is impossible to read the inscription. It would have given the distance from Castle Lock to Trent Lane Lock 1¼ miles.

On leaving the lock, the canal turns slightly left and then back to the right before running straight for a short distance. Approximately 25m above Castle Lock an overflow passes under the towpath, draining water from the canal into a small brook known as Tinkers Leen. Two large underground pipes then carry the water away to the river Trent. The overflow was not easy to cross for many years. Horses would walk through the water while the boatman walked on planks

A canal scene in Nottingham in 2004. The entrance to Fellows Morton & Clayton Wharf and warehouse is on the right.

Wilford Street Bridge on the left with the Navigation Inn at the back of the buildings behind. Narrow boats were taken down and a new building was built by the Trent Navigation Co., later taken over by British Waterways; the dateis unknown. (Nottingham County Library Local History Department)

Above: The Trent Navigation Co. building that replaced the old wharf in the picture at the bottom of page 102. The date is unknown. (Nottingham County Library Local History Department)

Right: Scene from Wilford Street Bridge. Three Trent barges are outside the British Waterways Building. The date is unknown. (Nottingham County Library Local History Department)

Above: Scene looking east in the direction of Wilford Street; the canal has a good head of water, but luckily only the horse got wet feet from the overflow which carried water into a small river called Tinkers Leen. The date is unknown. (Nottingham County Library Local History Department)

Left: Castle Lock No.2, taken in 1976, now the only surviving lock on the canal, apart from Trent Lock, to lower the canal into the river.

No.2 plate in Castle Lock wall, below the bottom gates.

A mile post at the side of Castle Lock. It once said '1¼ Miles to the Trent'; now only the words remain, the milestone having worn away over the years. This was taken in 2004.

just above the water. The procedure was helped in 1982 when the towpath was improved. A new footbridge was opened in 2004, much wider and with railings. On the towpath side for some distance were Kings Meadow railway sidings and many warehouses built by London, Midland & Scottish Railway Co. A much smaller building close to the sidings was once used by A.H. Garner Canal Iron Works, the name in large letters across the roof. These buildings have, over the last few years, been demolished and replaced with modern ones.

The building close to the lock is owned by Yorkshire Bank. At the side of this building is an old cast-iron parish boundary marker, dated 1869, with names of overseers of the poor, responsible for administrating the infamous Poor Law. The area once occupied by the railway sidings is now a very large retail park with a Sainsbury's close to Castle Meadow Moorings, useful for boaters wishing to do some shopping. Mooring time is forty-eight hours maximum. Good access to the canal is available all along this section of canal.

Opposite the towpath above Castle Lock, there have been many changes over the years. All the wharves and canal buildings have gone. The first building of interest is Vyella House, originally designed by Frank Broadhead in 1932 for William Hollins & Co., manufacturers of vyella fabrics, who at the time were one of the largest textile manufacturers in Nottingham. It was one of the first buildings to be built using concrete mushroom-shaped headed columns, restored in 1987–88 by James McArthey Partnership. It now houses the offices of Bass Leisure.

Following this come two very smart blocks of flats overlooking the canal. The first block has large balconies taking advantage of the view. The second block is set a little further back with a well-cut front lawn with a pond and fountain. Both were built in recent years. Occupying this area before was a small brewery, car sales depot and a little red-brick building which in early days acted as the canal company's stables. All these new flats have their entrances on Castle Boulevard, as did the earlier buildings. A footbridge now passes over the canal from Castle Boulevard to the retail park on the other side, also giving access to the towpath. Once past the footbridge, the canal turns to the left and is only a short distance from Castle Boulevard which runs parallel for a while.

Back to the towpath side, just after the footbridge, Tinkers Lean disappears, having been close to the towpath since Castle Lock. The towpath is excellent here, with mooring rings and block paving. (A word here about the many cyclists who use the towpath for access into Nottingham – take care, as they seem to appear from behind you without making a sound! Very few have bells fitted these days.)

The canal runs straight again here. A towpath bridge is next over the entrance to Castle Marina. Work started on the marina in 1981; it opened early in 1982 and passing boats have access to everything they need in this area. It also has a good chandlery for spares and so on. Close to its entrance on the left side is the Exchange Diner, where good food is available and tables and chairs are positioned outside overlooking the canal. It gets very busy here, due in a large part to its very pleasant location.

Cast-iron boundary marker dated 1869 showing names of overseers to the poor. This can be found close to Castle Lock.

A Trent Barge travelling up the canal above Castle Lock, owned by a company from Newark on Trent called Cafferata & Co. The date is unknown. (Nottingham County Library Local History Department)

After Castle Marina, the canal turns slightly right before taking a long left turn. There are some more flats opposite the towpath where Castle Boulevard turns right away from the canal. The next bridge is a railway bridge built by Midland Counties Railway in the 1850s. It was built with three spans, the first one 34ft (10.370m), the second 32ft 9in (9.988m) and the third 32ft 7in. (9.938m). Each one is the same height at 9ft 7in (2.920m). The towpath is still excellent with plenty of mooring rings. There are some factories on both sides here followed by Lenton Lane Road Bridge, the last on the navigable section. Opposite the towpath now comes Trevithicks Boatyard with many boats moored up. They have a dry dock that can be booked, and during the summer months they run trip boats at the Victoria Embankment on the river Trent. The trips are always busy and seem popular.

The canal bears right just after the boat yard as it comes up to the junction with Beeston Cut. The river Leen, which comes down the old canal bed at this point, now passes under the canal on its way to join the river Trent. This junction used to veer sharply away from the Beeston Cut but is now banked up, making it impossible to see over to where the canal once was from water level. On inspection of the ground over this bank, some large canal towpath masonry blocks can be found in the undergrowth. Anyone passing here now, whether on the towpath or in a boat, would surely never realise that the canal once turned off in that direction, climbing through a further seventeen locks in approximately 3½ miles.

8

LENTON CHAIN TO LOCK No.19

At Lenton Chain (as it was known locally) where the Nottingham Canal and Beeston Cut merged, there are few signs left to indicate a junction ever existed. It was here that the Nottingham Canal turned in a northerly direction. The towpath bridge that carried the Nottingham Canal towpath over the junction was removed many years ago and both waterways now appear as one. Leaving the Beeston Cut behind, it is only a short distance to Abbey Bridge, the A453 into Nottingham. When first built it was a brick-arch type canal bridge. The towpath was still on the left side after passing over the entrance of Beeston Cut. From here, between Abbey Street and Derby Road, the river Leen follows the route of the canal. Under Abbey Bridge there are some remains of the old canal towpath and just a short distance from this bridge is the site of Leathermill Lock No.3, of which no remains can be found. From here the canal turned slightly to the right before going into a straight section of about 400m up to Derby Road. On the left side now is the Queens Medical Hospital. It is still possible to walk up this side where the towpath was. The next bridge once was Leen Gate, an iron girder and wood structure. It is no longer there, having been removed many years ago. The road is now flat and still leads to Leen Gate, and is one of the entrances to the hospital. On the opposite side here are small industrial units and a lot of car parks. Also on this side from Abbey Street is a good wide pathway which is used for cycle path No.6 round Nottingham it keeps to that side until Leen Gate where it crosses back to the old towpath side until Derby Road. The cycle route heads in a northerly direction for Wollaton Park, Beechdale and Bilborough, also in a southerly direction for Lenton and then westerly for Beeston and Chilwell.

From where the cycle route crosses over at Leen Gate, the canal followed the line of Hill Side, and after about 200m from the junction with Derby Road the river Leen turns off to the right, leaving the canal behind. The canal bed here has been built over with yet another car park, followed by The Angels By Day Nursery which has a lovely grassy play area. Just before Derby Road Bridge, which was No.9, is a small piece of ground. This is the old canal bed which goes up to the bridge entrance, the entrance bricked up with a door in it. When it was bricked up, the original arch shape of the bridge was retained. The road is now many times wider than the old canal bridge would have been and is the A52 into Nottingham.

Derby Road is easy to cross by a push-button-operated crossing; once across the bridge, a long wall built of large pieces of masonry is visible. This is the top of the other side of the canal bridge, below which can be seen the other arched entrance to the bridge, also bricked up. As the canal came from under the bridge, Wollaton Park wall came down from the side of the park gatehouse to the side of the towpath. This wall was at the side of the towpath all the way up to Radford Bridge, No.10, which is now the main A609 into Nottingham. The wall was about 6ft high and was the original boundary of Wollaton Park. The park was the property of the Willoughby family. When the canal was built they would not allow it to cross their land, hence the reason for the canal being built around the outside of this wall. Just to the left of the bridge, standing proudly, is the gatehouse. This was the old entrance into the park before it was purchased by Nottingham Corporation in 1925; after purchase, the park was reduced in size by the corporation and some parts were used for housing. The gatehouse no longer gives direct access into the park.

An old entrance between two rows of iron leading down to the canal towpath are still to be found on the left side, only a short distance from the site of Hicklings Lock, No.4, at Radford Marsh. To the left of these railings, on a fenced-off piece of ground, can be found an old hand-operated water pump. It is possible this pump could have been installed to supply water for passing boat families. A little further on, also on the side once occupied by the towpath, can be found among some trees a quantity of large masonry blocks, very close to the where the lock was, which could be from the lock chamber. It was built using this type of block.

On this section from the A52 at Lenton to the A609 at Radford Bridge, a distance of half a mile, there was also Lock No.5, Simpson's. The canal ran straight between lock nos 4 and 5. On the canal bank opposite the towpath between the locks was one of the canal company's toll houses. After passing Lock No.5 it turned sharply left and ran straight for a short distance before turning right through Radford Bridge. In the late 1940s, this section – Lock No.5 up to Radford Bridge – was always very shallow and was known as the part of the canal where the bottom was floating on top. The reason for the shallowness in later years, after the canal had been abandoned, was most likely the coal wharf. For many years a lot of coal dust and fine coal must have fallen into the water, which must have made it silt up more quickly. The wharf was Radford Coal Wharf, used for distributing coal around Radford and loading coal from Radford Colliery. Coal came down to the wharf by a small tramway; this, though, has long gone and has now been built over by factories once used by Raleigh Industries. Also on this pound, before the coal wharf, was another for the sewage works. Sewage was collected on carts from local areas and taken to the works. Boats loaded with waste were then taken down the canal, to the larger works. There is nothing left of the canal here. Nottingham 62nd Scout Group has its headquarters built across the canal bed, followed by Charnock Avenue Playing

Fields. The line of canal can be followed by walking along Orston Drive. The house here used to back onto the canal towpath.

The remains of Lock No.6 can be found at the junction of Radford Bridge Road and the main A609 at Wollaton. The entrance to the lock came straight after the bridge with very little distance separating them. Part of the lock entrance wall, towpath side, can be found, clearly showing its large No.6 plate still fixed to it. The small section of canal that passed under the A609 has been filled in at roughly canal level and made into an underpass for pedestrians. The bridge is much the same as it was when the canal passed under it, although it is not the first bridge that was built, having been changed and made wider with road improvements over the years. The original bridge was a brick arch with a span of 22ft 2in (6.764m), with access to the towpath on both sides. These have been retained to give access to the underpass.

It was in the pound above Lock No.6 where the company had its maintenance yard and workshop. This pound between locks 6 and 7 was almost as wide as it was long and seemed to have been purpose-built at time of the canal's construction, with the pound being so wide it came up to the side of Radford Bridge Road, the overflow from Lock No.7 Limekiln, instead of emptying just below where the lock was piped into the corner of the pound, so as not to cause any water disturbance down the centre. It also included a dry dock to carry out boat repairs. Located in an ideal place for a maintenance yard, being in the heavy locked section approximately 2½ miles from the river Trent and 2¾ miles from Wollaton top lock, all locks were in this first 5¼ miles. This would have been where most of the maintenance was needed. There was an entrance to the yard by road from Radford Bridge Road so some supplies could be taken that way. All this area has changed completely. There is no visible sign of the canal anywhere. The canal was piped here in 1956 and levelled to the height of Lock No.6 top gates. The site of Lock No.6 is now a car park for small businesses built on the land once occupied by the maintenance yard, followed by a small housing development on West Hay Court.

I remember looking through the fence of this yard many times as a boy on my way to school and seeing all the piles of wood, some which were most probably stop planks, although by that time the gates were always padlocked and the yard appeared deserted, this section of canal having been abandoned some years earlier. On a point of reminiscence, I remember once going fishing in the river Trent during school holidays – I would have been about thirteen years old at the time – and catching a roach about ½lb in weight. So pleased was I that I wrapped it up in a damp cloth to take home. On arriving home it was still alive so it was put in a bath full of water. It was still alive three days later. Feeling sorry for it, having watched its fight to live, I put it in a bucket of water and carried it all the way to the canal, putting it in the pound between lock nos 6 and 7. For some years after, when passing the area, I wondered what happened to that fish and whether or not it survived. At the time I had a cat and it had been my original intention to give the fish to the cat for tea. At least the cat didn't know what he had missed.

The canal bed below Lock No.18. The towpath was alongside the hedge on the right, the high ground from the left to the centre is the remains of Wollaton Colliery slag heap. It was in this area that some scenes for the film *Saturday Night Sunday Morning* were filmed.

Wollaton Lock No.19 with the colliery in the background. This was taken in 1961. (Peter Stevenson)

Filled-in canal bed above Lock No.19 at Wollaton. The towpath ran down the side of the hedges on the left at the rear of the gardens on Welwyn Road. Bilborough Cut entered the main line here on the right.

On the site of Lock No.7 is Wollaton House, a children's home, which is followed by Seaford Avenue children's playground, the canal bed having been filled and grassed for a play area. There is a pathway from Radford Bridge Road across the playground to Seaford Avenue in roughly the same place as the one once used when crossing the top of Lock No.7 to access the towpath. Taking this path from Radford Bridge Road direction the canal was at the rear of the houses on the right. Nothing indicates now that a canal once passed that way. Also in this area, approximately 250m above Lock No.7 on the right canal bank, opposite the towpath, was Jackie Mathew's farm and Lime Kilns. It stood there for many years, closing down approximately seventy years ago. My father, a keen gardener, could remember going to get lime from there for his garden in 1928–30 and believes it closed down around that time. The top gates

This photograph was taken twenty years later than the picture on page 113, in 1996, looking in the opposite direction down Torvill Drive. The hedges at the rear of gardens on Welwyn Road can still be seen on the right, following the line of canal towpath. Lock No.19 would have been behind houses just beyond the car in the centre.

A small inlet between properties on Torvill Drive, Wollaton. The line of trees between them was once part of the hedge along the towpath below Lock No.17.

of the lock were used frequently by people to cross the canal, as a path led to it from Radford Bridge Road, making it an easy access point to the towpath. From here the canal ran straight for a short distance before taking a left turn followed by a short straight on the run up to Black Lock No.8. This is part of the canal, which was piped leaving no trace of the locks which passed the houses on Charlbury Road, Wollaton, from lock nos 8 to 13, including the first flight of three, lock nos 9, 10 and 11. The canal ran straight, on the flight of three, pounds between were oval shaped with masonry walls on both sides. Taking a walk down Charlbury Road is a good way to follow the line of the canal. From the remains of Lock No.6 nothing is left of the canal until Lock No.14, at the side of Lambourne Drive, Wollaton.

Before leaving this area I would like to reminisce just a little about the place where I lived and spent my boyhood days. My parents and I lived on Manville Close off Radford Bridge Road. They lived there for forty-five years. This was only a short walk from the canal, under the railway bridge and down Radford Bridge Road, passing Radford Woodhouse on the left with its rows of back-to-back houses on Gate Street, Vane Street and Lever Street where many of the local coal miners lived, working at both Wollaton and Radford Collieries. On Gate Street the nearest building to the railway was Kirk's Shop. I visited it many times for groceries as it was the closest shop to our house. An old shop with goods stacked everywhere and only a small counter, there was only a small space inside for shoppers. All non pre-packed items were weighed out in the required amount and put in paper bags. Many customers would have goods through the week, Mr Kirk keeping a book, with the customer also having a copy. This would then be paid up at the end of each week, after pay day which was usually Friday. Radford Woodhouse is no longer there, having been demolished to make way for newer properties.

Further down on the right side, which would be opposite the towpath on the canal, was Jackie Mathew's Farm. He farmed the land along the canalside past lock nos 8, 9, 10, 11 and 12 as well as some of the land on which Charlbury Road was built.

Across Radford Bridge Road from Manville Close, for many years there was a row of houses known locally as Engine Town. It was demolished some time before the Second World War. After the war was over, when there was a need for housing, the local council's solution was to build single-storey pre-fabricated houses for rent, which became known as 'prefabs'. I understand these properties were only intended for short-term use – around ten years – but they were there for something like thirty years.

Opposite the junction of Radford Bridge Road and Beechdale Road, there was a footpath from Beechdale Road to Aspley Lane known as Colliers Pad. It was in this area that we played our games. The name Colliers Pad originated from when coal miners, or colliers as they were known locally, walked that way to work. Many of the Nottinghamshire colliers, after a shift down the mine, would go to the allotment where they would grow vegetables, rear pigs and have a pigeon loft

Bridge at Wollaton in 1946. Note the pair of stop gates. The towpath still appears in fine condition nine years after being abandoned. (R. Berry)

from which they would take part in races, which my own uncle did when he was a collier down Radford Colliery. Scrap food would be collected to feed the pigs until just before Christmas, when they would be slaughtered at the local abattoir and everyone who contributed the scrap food would receive a piece of pork. Following Colliers Pad from the Beechdale Road end on the left was Cherry Orchard, a flat area where we played football and cricket. Across from this on the right was Humps and Hollows. A complete contrast to Cherry Orchard, it was good for war games and cowboys and Indians, comprising as it did a mass of raspberry canes and undergrowth. I've picked many a jar of raspberries there.

Standing at the side of Colliers Pad, partly in a ditch between Cherry Orchard and Humps and Hollows, stood the tallest elm tree I have ever seen. This great tree could be seen for miles. It had a very wide trunk with hardly any branches at the bottom, making it impossible to climb. People would come for miles just to see this wonderful tree. I last saw it in the 1950s. I had left home to join the Regular Army and was away a few years, and on returning home one of the first things I noticed was that the great elm had gone, the area having been claimed for housing. Colliers Pad later became Redbourne Drive. I have always thought it a great shame that during the developments and the naming of the new streets no mention was made to this great elm tree. After all, it stood there for many years dominating all around it.

The site of Lock No.13 is under the section of Lambourne Drive that goes up to where it leads to East Midlands Electricity Board Training Facility and meets

Taken from under the bridge in the previous picture, looking down the canal in the direction of Bramcote Moor in 1946. (R. Berry)

Woodyard Lane. This lock is of particular interest as it was the place where the pipe laying started. The top entrance to the lock had a grill set in a sloping front wall; this had been built to allow water from the canal above to enter the lock. From its appearance, the wall could have been built with lock masonry stones from other demolished locks. The grill was made from cast iron, similar to those found at the side of roads to take water away into the drains. The lock chamber had been concreted over at the level of the walls and three inspection covers had been fitted in the top, making it possible to see inside if required, and giving it the appearance of a large manhole. At the time this work was done, the grill was intended to allow water to remain in the canal above Lock No.13. By the mid-1970s this part of the canal had also dried up, all water supplies having been cut off. It was now starting to be used for dumping of all manner of things: unwanted cars, fridges, beds, cycles – you name it and people dumped it. There is now no evidence of all the changes made at Lock No.13. The pound in between lock nos 13 and 14 for many years had a tree growing out of the wall opposite the towpath, the roots lifting some large masonry blocks. Hallowell Drive has been built over this area, removing all traces of the canal.

Many years ago here on Woodyard Lane, close to the canal, was Brown's Sawmill, a well-known local timber merchant employing about twelve men. It was a family business supplying wood products to the building industry around Nottingham. I don't believe any of the timber was transported by narrow boat along the canal and there was never a wharf for boats in the area of Lock No.13. At that time, Woodyard Lane was just a track passing over both canal and railway. The Wollaton Road end has been taken over by Lambourne Drive while the rest remains largely the same, leading out onto the traffic island at the junction of Wigman Road and Hollington Road.

From lock nos 13 to 19 the canal was in the same condition in the 1970s, dried-up bed with some remains of all the locks, from the complete chamber of No.17 to just side walls in some cases and bits and pieces of others. In order going up: nos 14 and 15 were almost complete, No.16 has just the front entrance full of rubbish, Lock No.18's front entrance walls are visible, and Lock No.19's chamber is filled in up to the top of the walls. Since the 1980s all these locks have slowly been completely removed and built over with the exception of lock nos 14 and 15 which appear to have been partly demolished and filled in. After the remains of Lock No.15 can be found the complete pound between lock nos 15 and 16. The pound is oval in shape with all walls showing and the base made flat and grassed over. This is now the only remains of the Wollaton Flight of locks. It can be found at the junction of Torvill Drive and Lambourne Drive by going through the gate in the fence on the right side at the top end of Lambourne Drive. The site of Lock No.16 would have been under the road opposite this fence. From the mid-1970s until all the new developments were built, the area around the entrance to this lock was an awful sight with a great deal of rubbish left there. I was there one day when a car drove up and a man got out, emptied three cases of his rubbish on top of the rest and drove away. The bridge just in front of the lock was Coach Road No.12. Old Coach Road, as it is known, can still be found on both sides of Lambourne Drive. Here, on both sides of the canal, Raleigh Cycle Co. had their sports ground. The factory was for many years on Faraday Road in Radford, not all that far from the canal.

To the next lock: Lock No.17 was in a straight line from Lock No.16, a distance of about a quarter of a mile. Immediately turning sharply left on leaving the lock, the canal was then straight for another third of a mile before again turning right into the entrance of Lock No.18. Along both these two pounds on the towpath side there was a slight embankment, dropping approximately 2m into the field below, which was full of many allotments. Just before entering Lock No.18, the embankment on the towpath side levelled out to give way to a hedgerow at the rear of houses on Ewell Road. Opposite the towpath on the pound in between lock nos 17 and 18 was the remains of Wollaton Colliery slag heap. (It was in this area in 1960 that some of the film 'Saturday Night Sunday Morning', staring Albert Finney, Shirley Anne Field and Thora Hird, was filmed.) The pound in between lock nos 18 and 19 was once again only small, with Wollaton Colliery close to the side opposite the towpath. Wollaton Colliery closed in 1963. It was a number of years before the slag was removed.

The canal reached its summit level at Lock No.19, having climbed 133ft (40.56m) in the first 5¼ miles from the river Trent. Once the canal reached its summit level, it was at the 200ft contour where it remained for all 9½ miles to Langley Mill, traversing round the eastern side of the Erewash Valley.

The houses on Torvill Drive have their gardens mostly on the canal bed all the way along, except for just one small break in the houses on the left side, after its junction with Lambourne Drive, which shows a small row of trees. These trees are part of the hedge, running alongside the towpath between lock nos 16 and 17.

9

THE TOP POUND

Surveying the start of the top pound above Lock No.19, it is strange to think a canal ever passed through these housing estates. The top end of Torvill Drive was laid on the canal bed. Barnham Close, off Torvill Drive, is also built over what was once canal bed and part of Lock No.19. (On Torvill Drive, almost opposite Barnham Close, is Dean Close. Both Torvill Drive and Dean Close were named after the popular ice dancers from Nottingham.) Looking down Torvill Drive here, on the left side in the direction of Trowell Road (A609), can be seen hedgerows at the bottom of gardens on Welwyn Road. This hedge is the same that was at the side of the canal towpath. The canal ran straight here from above Lock No.19 to Trowell Road, a distance of about 200m.

It was here, just above the lock, that hot water emptied into the canal from Wollaton Colliery. As mentioned earlier, it was a great place for swimming, known as 'Hotties' because of the warm water. I once caught a nice perch here, weighing 2lb – it seems the fish also liked warm water.

Just above Lock No.19, the Bilborough Cut left the main line. Passing close to the Wollaton Colliery, it ran level to a wharf close to Bilborough Wood and was joined by tramroads from Bilborough and Strelley Collieries. It was a private venture built by local landowners, opened three years after the Nottingham Canal. Unfortunately, it only had a short life. The Bilborough end was disused by 1813 whilst a small section close to the main line was kept open as wharves until the mid-1870s.

From Trowell Road the canal follows a long right turn then straightens out in a deep cutting as it approaches Coventry Lane Bridge, Stapleford (A6002). This road was for many years a minor road, having been widened and upgraded in recent years to 'A' status. Were a bridge still in existence it would have a No.16 plate fastened to it. Before reaching this bridge, on the aforementioned right turn, there was Stackyard Bridge No.14 and Bramcote Moor No.15, which was a high bridge halfway down the cutting. At its highest point this cutting would have been about 20ft (6.1m) above canal level. The line of canal from Trowell Road to Coventry Lane passed through an area now covered by a number of streets and

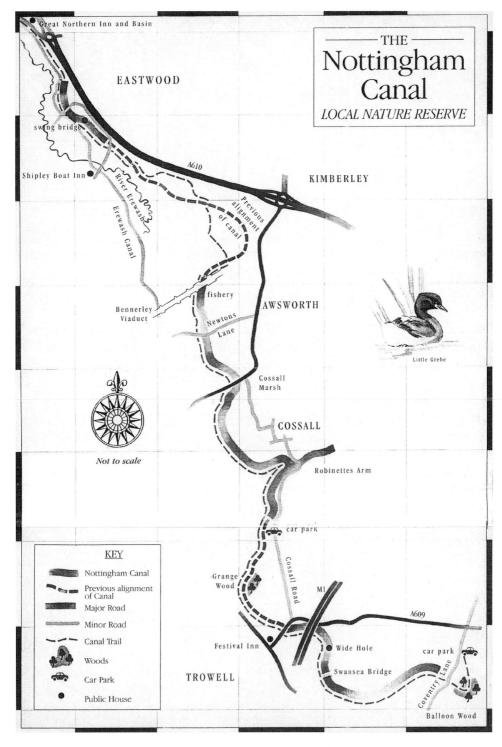

Map showing the section of the canal now owned by Broxtowe Borough Council. It is now a nature reserve. Reproduced by kind permission of the council. (Broxtowe Borough Council)

a school, as follows: Trowell Road, Greenwood Road, across Fernwood School grounds, Fernwood Crescent, Rushmore Avenue, Wollaton Vale, Edlington Drive, Grangewood Road and Latimer Drive.

Just before reaching Bridge No.16 there is a small stretch of canal under a railway bridge where a small amount of water can still be found alongside some remains of the towpath.

Leaving Bridge No.16 behind, the canal is found once again, this part owned by Broxtowe Borough Council. A new sign has been put up by the council, stating, 'Nottingham Canal Nature Reserve'. There is also a good fenced-off parking area put in by the council. The ground slopes down from this car park for about 150m, where it reaches canal level and a little water can be found. There is no other water along this section, which is approximately 1¼ miles; the canal bed turns in a long left bend with little twists and turns within it before turning back right where it comes to a stop at Trowell Garden Centre, which occupies the canal bed for a short distance. All the rest of this section is very overgrown with many trees in the canal bed. It is an excellent towpath all the way and well maintained. Things of interest to look for include some narrows, where a good canal wall is to be found on both sides with cast-iron inserts for stop planks. This is followed by an overflow weir to take water from the canal. It was built opposite the towpath and is now much higher than the canal bed. Water hasn't flowed over it for many years. Potter's Bridge, a very nice masonry-built bridge, No.17, comes next and appears to have been repointed in recent years, followed by a much overgrown winding hole. Opposite here, where railway and canal come close, was the site of Trowell Moor Colliery. Towpath walling can be picked out, giving a good idea of what depth of water used to be in the canal. All along here the canal was dug out of the hillside with an embankment starting at approximately 1m, rising to 5m from fields below. The canal now stops at Trowell Garden Centre and a footpath leads off to the left and goes round the garden centre back to the canal on the other side. Another footpath goes left over the railway through Stapleford and Bramcote hills back to the canal via Bramcote Moor, passing a local landmark en route – the Hemlockstone – a tall sandstone outcrop 6.6m high, believed to have been used for practising witchcraft. This stone derives its name from the poisonous hemlock plant nearby.

The canal starts again once past Trowell Garden Centre with about half a mile length that stops again when it comes up against the M1. It starts with Swansea Bridge, No.18, which is in good condition with the remains of a pair of stop gates slowly rotting away in the bridge hole. Where the towpath passes through, boards have been put across to stop anyone entering the garden centre this way. It's dry here and overgrown for a quarter of a mile, then a winding hole appears, full of clear, deep water marked by a warning sign put up by Broxtowe Council informing walkers of the depth. From Swansea Bridge the canal takes a right turn up to this winding hole, after which it runs straight to the M1 on an embankment on both sides. At its highest point this embankment is approximately 10m above the road, below the A609 Nottingham Road, Trowell. Trowell village was chosen for the Festival of Britain in 1951 and just a short walk from the canal is Festival Inn, which takes its name from this event, having opened some time later. It is a fine watering hole and good for refreshments. The name Trowell is believed to come from 'Tree by the well'; there were six wells in the village a century ago.

Across the other side of the motorway is just a short stretch of canal about 250m long before it comes to a stop at Nottingham Road, and what would have been Bridge No.19. This bridge has changed many times in recent years with the widening of the A609. When first built, it was a masonry arch the same as No.18. It was on this small section that Nottingham Canal Society helped with repairs in 1979 when the canal breached. Repairs were carried out at the request of Broxtowe Borough Council. Work was done by building a wall across the full width of canal, just past the breach, approximately 50m from the motorway. A line of pipes were then laid in the canal bed from this wall up to a pipe which carried water under the motorway to the canal on the other side. A small overflow was then built in the wall to carry water into these pipes when water reached overflow level. The ground around the pipes was then filled in and levelled. Repairing the breach in this way reduced pressure on the canal bank while keeping water in the canal on both sides of the motorway. The canal bank was then rebuilt and towpath repaired. The towpath is good on both these sections and easy to reach down a signed footpath from the A609, close to Bridge No.19. Where the motorway passes over the canal, it is necessary to walk down the embankment and under the motorway from each side to gain access back onto the towpath.

Once through this last bridge, the towpath continues without the canal for approximately a mile, the canal having been infilled to towpath level. It was necessary to infill this section owing to the weakness of canal banking in the areal; if left water could possibly have breached causing damage to properties below canal level.

Retained along this section are a series of four ponds, one utilising the former site of Marriots swing bridge, No.20, with the others adjacent to Grange Wood. There was a small cutting on leaving the bridge with the higher ground leading away opposite the towpath as the canal followed a right turn along the contour. It was only a short distance to where land started to fall away on the towpath side, this slowly becoming higher the further the canal progressed up the valley. Higher ground continues for most of the way on the one side with a wooded area known as Grange Wood coming down to the canalside. The towpath hedge is still in place all along, making it easy to follow the canal's route. There are good views across the Erewash Valley from here. A short distance from the end of this right turn, the high ground opposite the towpath levels out but the fields on the towpath side still drop away.

Cossall Road is now close, coming from the right opposite the towpath. This a good place to start a walk along the Erewash Valley, taking in the canal at the same time. Good car parking is once again provided by Broxtowe Borough Council, positioned over the end of the infilled section and signed at the side of Cossall Road 'Nottingham Canal Nature Reserve'; from here the canal is in water again.

It keeps close to the road here for about half a mile, making little turns left and right up to its junction with Robbinetts Arm. There is a narrow footbridge over from a small parking area at the road side about 300m from the previous parking area. The canal narrows here; this could possibly have been the site of a swing bridge or a location for stop gates. From here there is a slight turn to the right up to the junction of Robbinetts Arm as it winds its way round the hillside.

The Robbinetts Arm is now the only arm remaining, all the others having been destroyed over a number of years for various reasons. On approaching the junction Robbinetts Arm carried straight on, passing under a swing bridge (long since gone), possibly No.21, the main line turning sharp left. This arm is 3 furlongs in length and contains a reasonable amount of water. Opened the same time as the main line, it was served by tramways from collieries to wharves close to its terminus. Important as one of the canal's main water supplies, water culverted down from ponds in Oldmoor Wood about 1 mile to the west, entering at the top end of the arm. Cossall Road is on a sharp bend just above the junction where the swing bridge used to be.

From the sharp left turn taken by the main line it is only a short distance up to Cossall Embankment, which carries the canal across another valley that enters the Erewash Valley on its east side. It's not a very wide valley but the embankment is approximately 35 to 40ft high on both sides of the waterway and looks very high from Cossall Road, below which it runs. The embankment has been cleaned out but contains a little water, however, as with most of the canal in this area. Once over this short valley the canal again takes another sharp left turn along the contour with high ground on the right and a steep drop into the valley below the towpath side. Once again there are good views over the Erewash Valley to Ilkeston on the far side. After the second bend it's only about 150m to the site of another swing bridge. Now long gone, it has been replaced with a footbridge. Although the swing bridge has disappeared, the stonework which supported it is clear to see.

Leaving the towpath here and following the footpath across this footbridge to Cossall Village is well worth the walk. The footpath crosses Mill Lane before reaching Church Lane; turn right here down Church Lane into the village on the left and you will see some almshouses built in 1685 by George Willoughby. Across the road from the school is Church Cottage, once the home of Louise Burrows, fiancée of D.H. Lawrence, novelist, playwright, poet and artist. Cossall is a very attractive village that was designated a conservation area as part of European Architectural Year in 1975. At the bottom of Church Lane turn right into Mill Lane back to the canal; this can be done in two ways: by rejoining the footpath again halfway down the lane or carrying on to the bottom and joining at the next canal bridge. This bridge is also a swing bridge, a strong-looking structure. At its side are the remains of a pair of stop gates. From the previous footbridge to the swing bridge the canal takes a right turn around the side of the hill.

The canal runs straight now for about 200m, containing water all the way, with a reasonably clear channel. It twists and turns for three quarters of a mile to where the remains of Old Cossall Colliery Drift used to be, previously the drift from

Bennerley Viaduct across the Erewash Valley; this viaduct spanned both Nottingham and Erewash canals as well as the river Erewash. It is now a listed structure.

Oakwood Grange Colliery. Oakwood Grange Colliery closed in February 1957 after a connection was made between Oakwood Grange and Cossall collieries in 1953. The workforce at Oakwood Grange was transferred to Cossall and Cossall Colliery closed, thirteen years after the connection was made, in November 1966. The remains of two stop gates can be found in front of the drift, now well rotted.

The canal now bears to its right for a short distance with the ground levelling out on both sides; it is not long before it takes a left turn and there is level ground only on the right, the towpath side is again built up with a 3–4m drop to the ground below. This is the site of what appears to have been another swing bridge which has been replaced with a much narrower footbridge. In front of this the canal is filled in with a pipe through to keep water at the same level on both sides. Horses cross here from the towpath to a footpath at the other side, but a sign by the footbridge says 'no horses'. In the 1970s the towpath was blocked off with a notice board warning people to 'Keep Off' as ground around here was smouldering. The ground here below the canal embankment was for some years the site of Cossall Colliery, previously Hewlett Pit. There were a number of small black mounds all over the area about 2m high, just like small slag heaps of very fine coal. Looking at the smouldering that was going on at the time it would appear some burning was happening underneath. This meant leaving the towpath, climbing down the bank to bypass the area, rejoining the towpath on the other side. When collieries on the lower ground below the towpath closed it was used as railway sidings carrying coal from other collieries, still open. It has all changed again in recent years. The problem of the smouldering bank has been taken care of and the area is now an industrial park on Soloman Road off Coronation Road, Awsworth. There is a good place to eat on Coronation Road called Chatterley House Hotel with an excellent restaurant and good service.

It is just a short walk now to where the canal passes over Coronation Road, formerly the A6096 before Awsworth Bypass was built. By going down Soloman Road off Coronation Road into the industrial estate access to the canal towpath is from a path leading up the embankment. The railway bridge built for the sidings is still in place and now a footpath crossing Coronation Road at a lower level than the canal leads back up the embankment to reach towpath level.

The concrete structure here which was built to maintain the same water level on both sides of Coronation Road is now referred to locally as Nottingham Canal Aqueduct; when the canal was constructed no aqueduct was ever built here. It was a continuous embankment about 10m high. On inspection of this structure it is 2¼m wide with no solid bottom, the sides made of cast concrete. At each end of these pipes contained within the concrete sides are four large grilles to keep the pipe entrances clear from floating debris; this is no longer an issue as the water level is lower than the pipes. At the time of the canal's construction there was a brook here that came down from Babbington through Cossall Marsh down to the river Erewash, which was lower than the canal; it was culverted through the embankment.

The canal again at Awsworth with the Bennerley Viaduct in the background in 1991. (Broxtowe Borough Council)

Members of the National River Authority checking fish stocks at Newtons Lane, Awsworth, in 1992. (Broxtowe Borough Council)

Filled-in canal bed at Park Hill, Awsworth, in 1996.

A brick-built bridge over the dried-up canal bed at Awsworth in 1976; this bridge was demolished in the late 1980s.

On Ordnance Survey Maps for 1887 the brook is still shown as passing through the embankment at the point where the road is now. On a later map of 1921 the road is shown passing through the embankment at the same point. The brook must have been taken underground at the time the road was built because it is only shown on the north side of the embankment; where the road passes through it is shown as narrowing, only giving passage for single-file traffic. The canal is still shown at its full width passing over the road. The road, therefore, must have been put through some time between these two surveys. On present-day Ordnance Survey Maps it is shown by a break in the canal water line where it crosses over the road.

It is not certain when any changes were made in the embankment early on, but there was some trouble. In his *History of Ilkeston* (published by J.F. Walker of Ilkeston), Edwin Trueman mentions that in the year 1823 the embankment close to the aqueduct gave way, water coming down in torrents and completely flooding the low-lying houses in the immediate neighbourhood. By aqueduct he probably meant the culverted brook through the embankment at that time.

Dissatisfaction with the state of the embankment in the area of the aqueduct was apparent for many years. It was reported in the *Ilkeston Pioneer* on 26 January 1900 that the aqueduct was supported by timbers. At this time Basford Urban District Council were considering making a new public road through the embankment at the point of the aqueduct maintenance for the area was under their jurisdiction. The canal was now owned by the Great Northern Railway Co., who should have maintained the area, but they refused to aid the project. When it was renovated in the railway company's blue brick materials and regulated by a set of traffic lights, the tunnel was able to pass single-deck buses operated by Midland General Omnibus Co. It was dangerous for anyone on the narrow pavement along the western wall if they were caught in the tunnel at the same time as a bus came through. In July 1957 Nottinghamshire County Council accepted a tender from W&C French of £31,741 for the construction of a new Cossall aqueduct and colliery siding bridge. The above council had previously purchased 150 square yards of land under a compulsory order, although no owner of the land could be found; it was believed to be part of the old Wollaton, Trowell and Cossall estate of the late Lord Middleton sold by public auction in 1925. With the new aqueduct it would be possible for two-way traffic to pass through with room for double-decker buses, once the original single-lane tunnel controlled by traffic lights was demolished. Construction was expected to take about twenty-one months. These improvements were long overdue with increasing road traffic. It would also be safer for pedestrians to have a much wider pavement. There had been one serious accident in recent years when a youth on a cycle was hit by a bus, causing fatal injuries. It was believed at the inquest that the cyclist passed traffic lights on green on the Kimberley side, but had not passed through before they turned to green on the Ilkeston side to admit the bus. The bus driver did not see the cyclist because of the bulge in the tunnel wall.

The new aqueduct was opened on Wednesday afternoon on 22 October 1958. At the opening two drivers of Midland General Omnibus Company Ltd drove two buses through, one a double-decker, the other a single. It was expected that both types of bus would be used. The height of this new structure is 15ft 4in (4.7m); the span of the pipes 90ft (9.4m).

The building involved excavating 6,000 cubic yards of canal embankment and 800 cubic yards of brickwork and masonry from the sides of the previous tunnel, masonry from the demolished structure was utilised in building new retaining walls. Approximately 4 miles of high tension steel and 1,000 cubic yards of concrete were also used. Work started in September 1957 and was completed ahead of the expected time of twenty-one months without stopping traffic at any time.

The canal is now in the area of Cossall Marsh; this last 5 miles is well looked after with an excellent towpath but it would be nice to see a little more water in places. It carries on along the embankment for roughly 200m before giving way to level ground on both sides as it turns slightly to the left.

At the end of this left turn are the foundations of another bridge. From the foundations still in place it would appear it was built of masonry stones. Before the bridge opposite the towpath is what seems to have been a small wharf, now very dry and much overgrown with remains of a boat rotting away close by. A short distance from here is also a low wall which once supported a railway bridge across the canal that carried a branch line of London Midland & Scottish Railway to Babbington. It was mainly used for transporting coal and was partially dismantled by 1938.

The canal is now cut through by Shilo Way, the new A6096 Awsworth Bypass, the name Shilo taken from when the area was known as Shilo open-cast mining area. A set of pedestrian operated traffic lights have been put here for crossing over from one side of the canal to the other with a gate giving access to the towpath on both sides. This next section, having crossed the road, starts with an overgrown stretch of canal giving way to a very pleasant stretch of clear wide waterway and plenty of water. Opposite the towpath was a large car and lorry scrap yard; many years before it had been the site of Cossall Brickworks, a private company with a quarry and small tramway, probably using the canal for transporting bricks from the nearby wharf. A little further on are a number of cottages with their gardens on the canal side. For many years the remains of an old canal narrow boat lay in the water at the bottom of these gardens slowly rotting away. This section comes to an end at Newtons Lane where the next bridge used to be; this bridge was demolished many years ago. The canal narrows on both sides of the road where it approached the bridge, two large pipes pass under the road to keep water at the same level on both sides of Newtons Lane. On Newtons Lane, opposite the towpath, is another car park put in by Broxtowe Borough Council, making this a good access point for walking the towpath. This area of the canal was known locally in the early years as Top Cut as it was the higher of the two local canals. The Erewash Canal in the valley below is known as Bottom Cut. The next section between Newtons Lane and Park Hill is now called Willoughby Top Cut. When the canal was first built this area belonged to the estate of the Willoughby family. Their home was Wollaton Hall, built by Sir Francis Willoughby in 1588.

Once over Newtons Lane there is the best section of waterway to be found on the whole of the top pound It stretches for approximately half a mile and is used by Awsworth Angling Club, which has an eighty-strong membership who also look after the area including the towpath, which is marked out for fifty-eight fishing pegs some of which are for disabled anglers. The water is very clear and has a good depth with the canal at its full width for most of the way. When I visited the area in 1976, just before the start of the 1976–77 course fishing season, a group of people were standing in the canal about a metre from the towpath up to their knees in water clearing weeds. They were doing this very successfully with old bicycle wheels tied onto the ends of long pieces of rope, casting these wheels almost two thirds across the canal, allowing them to sink and then dragging them to back across bringing weeds and debris with them, a simple and very effective method of clearing a waterway. In April 1987 this short section of waterway was restocked with more than 600 fish, a mixture of roach, carp and bream. The fish were transported by road from Humberside. About 50m from the beginning of this section is Bridge Farm with its white painted wall forming part of the towpath boundary. Close to this wall there used to be a cast-iron distance sign which said '11¼ miles to the Trent'. The canal now comes to a stop just before Park Hill, once the site of another canal bridge built with reddish type house bricks. Although I can say what materials were used in its construction its not possible to give this bridge a number, as so many bridges have been destroyed. There are only two bridges remaining that still retain their numbers, Bridge No.1, first bridge in Nottingham, and Bridge No.36, last bridge at Langley Mill.

There are once again good views across the Erewash valley along this last section, with the canal still clinging to the hillside following the 200ft contour. After this last bridge at Park Hill the Bennerley Viaduct crosses the canal on its way to the other side of the valley, passing over both the river Erewash and Erewash Canal; before becoming redundant it carried the Great Northern Railway Radcliffe to Burton line.

This viaduct has been the subject of many local council meetings over a number of years in the early 1980s. Some groups wished to have it demolished, others preferred keeping it for future generations. Opened in 1877, it was built to a new design known as the 'Warren System', a wrought-iron lattice construction that minimised the weight over the ground. It had been found that the ground was unsuitable for a heavy brick structure due to old coal and ironstone workings. It was closed in 1968 following the closure of the Great Northern Railway shortly after the line was dismantled, leaving the viaduct isolated. It then came under the ownership of British Rail and cost them upwards of £30,000 a year to maintain just to prevent it from becoming dangerous – a large expense and nothing to show for it. The viaduct is in two local council's areas, a quarter in Erewash Borough Council and three quarters in Broxtowe Borough Council.

Looking in the direction of Giltbrook with the Great Northern Railway Viaduct in the distance in 1921; both canal and railway have succumbed to other developments. The A610 Eastwood Bypass follows the line of the viaduct.

They were faced with children playing on and around it, and a number of them were injured through climbing up its sides and falling. In September 1984 Erewash Borough Council admitted that if a trust fund could not be set up to preserve it the council would be unable to oppose an order to demolish it. In 1985 the Bennerley Viaduct Preservation Trust was set up, a meeting was called on 5 August the same year inviting members of Erewash Borough Council, Derbyshire County Council, Awsworth Parish Council and British Rail. Five years earlier British Rail had applied for permission to demolish it. The trust was hoping to get them to withdraw the demolition plan and agree to sell or lease it to them. Conservation groups fighting to save the structure had been offered £20,000 from English Heritage to help preserve it. At the same meeting it was agreed to look into ways of making access onto the viaduct more difficult for children. The conservationists won the day; it is now a Grade II listed structure.

In the 1970s just before where the viaduct passed over the canal there was a red brick canal bridge that had sunk so low it was impossible to walk under its arch. The arch had been supported with iron braces. At that time the canal bed was dry; it was only 4ft (1.219m) from the canal bed to the underside of the bridge arch. This sinking could have been caused by mining subsidence it was finally demolished during the Shilo open-cast mining operations.

From Park Lane all the way up to New Manleys Road South, New Eastwood, the canal disappears having been lost to open-cast coal mining. An approximate alignment has been maintained as a footpath, this path forming part of the extended walk aligning with the canal towpath at each end. On this section was the junction with the short private Greasley Branch, leaving the main line in the

The bed of the canal looking east from New Manleys Road South, New Eastwood; this path is a pleasant walk following the line of the canal.

Watered section of canal between New Manleys Road South and Tinsley Road, New Eastwood, photographed in December 1999.

Swing bridge between New Manleys Road South and Tinsley Road, Eastwood. This was taken in December 1999.

Swing bridge between New Manleys Road South and Tinsley Road, Eastwood, being cleaned up by volunteers with help from Broxtowe Borough Council in 1993. (Broxtowe Borough Council)

Nottingham Canal Society members at a working party rebuilding Tinsley Road Bridge, Eastwood, in 1978.

direction of Giltbrook that lies between Kimberley and Eastwood. A number of tramways joined this branch from various small collieries; the largest was Digby Colliery, now closed.

Over the other side of New Manleys Road South the canal re-appears for half a mile up to Tinsley Road, where it disappears once again. Although isolated, this is a good section of canal with some water and a fine swing bridge approximately halfway along. A footpath crosses on this bridge from further up New Manleys Road South en route to the Erewash Canal, just a short distance across the fields. The Erewash Canal is now closer to the Nottingham Canal than the river Erewash, the canal having passed over the river a short distance away down the valley. Now that only a narrow piece of land separates the two waterways, the Erewash Canal has just one more lock to pass through to reach the same 200ft contour as the Nottingham Canal.

The canal has also vanished from Tinsley Road to Derby Road, Langley Mill. This is the area of Bailey Grove. The canal twists and turns along this final section to its terminus at the Great Northern Basin. The route of the canal is a footpath that follows close to the line taken by the canal, laid by Broxtowe Borough Council and maintained by them.

There was a very unique bridge along this last section built with red-brick sides and a wooden top, the wooden top was flat with a cross pattern on the

Tinsley Road Bridge in 1996 after the canal had been filled in on both sides of bridge.

This picture was taken in 2004, some twenty-six years after rebuilding by members of Nottingham Canal Society. This view shows Tinsley Road Bridge, still in good condition.

outside. It was the penultimate bridge and only the second along the canal to be built to this design. Unfortunately, it was demolished some time in the late 1980s. This design of bridge was only built on the Nottingham Canal. The other one was demolished in the late 1960s. At the site of this bridge the footpath reaches Anchor Road, which must be followed up to Derby Road.

The building here on land close to both canals was once the Anchor Inn, which closed in the 1930s. In this area the two canals come closest to one another; the Nottingham Canal Society hoped to put in a lock to join both waterways, had the Nottingham Canal been restored. The Erewash Canal still has one more lock to negotiate before entering the Great Northern Basin. With Derby Road (A608) having cut through the Nottingham Canal it would have made it necessary to build a lock.

On the right along Derby Road (A608) and up the hill after passing over the Kimberley Bypass (A610) is the town of Eastwood whose most famous son was D.H. Lawrence, author, poet, playwright and artist, born on 11 September 1885 at 10 Victoria Street. Known locally with great affection as David Herbert, he died on 22 March 1936, aged forty-one. The house in Victoria Street where he was born is now a museum celebrating his life, though he only lived there until he was two. It is furnished in the style of a mining family of the early 1900s and some items have been added, such as his writing desk. The museum also contains some of his paintings. There is a small gift shop in the house next door from where the entrance to the museum is located. D.H. Lawrence was better known for his writing than anything else; his works included the controversial *Lady Chatterley's Lover*, which was banned. He also wrote books based on the area of his birth, of which he was very proud.

In Lawrence's book *The Rainbow*, the fictitious Brangwen family lived at Marsh Farm on Cossall Marsh, close to the canal. The farm – now demolished – stood between Church Lane and the canal a short distance from the junction of Church Lane and Coronation Road, the old A6096, before Shilo Way, the new Awsworth Bypass, was built. Lawrence enjoyed the canal and often gave it a mention in his writings. Moorgreen Reservoir, built by Nottingham Canal Co. for water supply, was referred to by Lawrence in his stories as Nethermere. He probably derived the name from a mixture of the word 'mere' (another name for a lake) and Nether Green Brook, the brook carrying water down to the canal from the reservoir.

The canal re-appears again on the other side of Derby Road. This short and final section is approximately 70m long. Though a short stretch, it widens out into a small basin that could have been a winding hole before passing its last bridge, a swing bridge in very good condition. The No.36 plate is still attached. It is possibly the only working bridge of its kind still in use. After passing this final bridge the canal enters the Great Northern Basin with the Erewash Canal entering on the left through its last lock. The last few metres of the canal is used for mooring crafts of various sizes. Each time one of these crafts needs to reach the moorings the crew must operate the restored swing bridge to gain entrance.

Just before this last section was the site of the stop lock, the last lock on the canal. It was closed in times of water shortage and is now under Derby Road. The Cromford Canal enters the basin facing the Nottingham and Erewash canals and is slowly being extended further away from the basin, now reaching about a quarter of a mile, containing many moored craft and a dry dock. The Great Northern

Left: The unique wooden top bridge at Bailey Grove near Langley Mill in 1976. This bridge was demolished a few years ago.

Below: Top end of Nottingham Canal at Langley Mill just before passing the last bridge, No.36, now used for moorings. This photograph was taken at a boat rally in 1989.

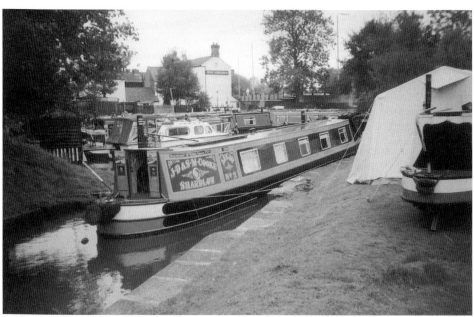

Opposite top: Moorings at No.125 still in use in 2004. This is the Great Northern Inn & Restaurant, centre.

Opposite middle: The Great Northern Basin in 1921, at the junction of the Nottingham, Cromford and Erewash canals. The Nottingham Canal came in through a swing bridge, No.36, just beyond the moored narrow boats, the Erewash Canal comes from the right and the Cromford Canal from the direction from which this picture was taken. The building behind the boats is the Tollhouse, shared by Nottingham & Cromford Cos. The Great Northern Inn is to the left of the Tollhouse.

Opposite bottom: Taken in 1976 from the Nottingham Canal entrance, this picture shows the same swing bridge with the tollhouse in the centre beyond the bridge. Only the first 150m of the Cromford Canal still retained water when this photograph was taken.

Left: The top end of the canal at Langley Mill, used for moorings. This was taken in 1976.

Below: Top lock on the Erewash Canal at Langley Mill as it enters the Great Northern Basin. Nottingham Canal comes in on the right behind the tent. This was 1996, a celebration arranged by The Erewash Canal Preservation & Development Association to celebrate Nottingham Canal's Bicentenary.

Basin does not have a regular water supply. The Erewash Canal Preservation & Development Association has installed a pump for pumping water back into the basin to keep the water level up.

The basin is very interesting. On leaving the Nottingham Canal behind, on the right side is the Nottingham Canal distance marker stating 14¾ miles to the Trent, a little further on is a small red-brick building which was used by both Nottingham and Cromford companies as their Toll Office.

Restoration of the Great Northern Basin was undertaken by the Erewash Canal Preservation & Development Association starting in 1971 and opened in 1973. The Great Northern Inn here stands at the side of the last few yards of the Nottingham Canal is well worth a visit and can be recommended for excellent

The bicentenary celebrations for the opening of the Nottingham Canal; Erewash Canal top lock is on the right. This was 1996.

food at a very reasonable price. An inn has stood here ever since the canals were built. According to Deborah Brown, the current landlady, many years ago it was called The Jawbone, the name coming from the shape formed by the Nottingham and Erewash canals as they entered the basin. Inside there is a large collection of photographs and mounted newspaper reports recording the re-opening of the basin and there is a mounted plaque on the land between the Nottingham and Erewash canals recording the re-opening event.

On the wall, mounted in a frame along with the photographs, is a copy of by-gone rules, which reads as follows:

RULES of the INN
NO Thieves, Fakirs, Rouges or Tramps.
NO Skulkers, Loafers or Flea Bittern Tramps.
NO Slap an Tickle O` The Wenches.
NO Banging O` Tankards on the Table.
NO Dogs Allowed in the Kitchen.
NO Cockfighting.

Flintlocks, Cudgels, Daggers & Swords
to be handed in to the Innkeeper for safe
keeping.

Bed for the night 1 Shilling
Stabling for horse 4 Pence
1786

Above: Great Northern Basin in 2004. Nottingham Canal is on the right, Erewash Canal on the left and Cromford Canal in the centre; it is now used for moorings and has a dry dock.

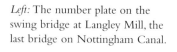

Left: The number plate on the swing bridge at Langley Mill, the last bridge on Nottingham Canal.

A mile post at the start of the Nottingham Canal at Langley Mill.

Commemorative plaque celebrating the re-opening of the Great Northern Basin. This was 2004.

Mileage plaque at the Great Northern Basin, showing a distance to Nottingham of 22 miles travelling via the Erewash Canal and river Trent.

The birth place of D.H. Lawrence in Eastwood, now a museum.

10

THE BEESTON CUT

This small but important waterway formed a link between the Nottingham Canal and the river Trent at Beeston. Most people nowadays seem to take the Beeston Cut and Nottingham Canal for the same waterway, when in fact they are completely different. Each one had its own engineer and Act of Parliament.

Having been dropped by the Nottingham Canal Co. in preference to its own route, Beeston Cut was not left to be forgotten. If one looks at the estimate submitted by William Jessop to the Nottingham Canal Co., it included a Beeston Meadow Branch at a cost of £4,750. I doubt very much that the actual line taken would have varied much between the one planned by William Jessop and the one taken when it received its own Act.

Work started on this 2½-mile waterway in 1794 and was completed in 1796. As early as July 1791 a letter was written to Nottingham Corporation, jointly by the Erewash Canal Co. and the Trent Navigation Co. asking for support in their effort to build a navigable cut to bypass the shallow and troublesome river Trent, but the corporation declined. It was known that the Erewash Canal Co. were not in favour of building the Nottingham Canal. Later, in September of the same year, members of the Nottingham Canal Co. committee attended a meeting held by the Trent Navigation Co. at which it was suggested the cut be made and that the Trent Navigation Co. contribute £2,000 towards the estimated of £5,000. The Nottingham Canal Co. also asked for 1d (5p) per boat making the through journey, as well as a water supply from the river Trent, the Trent Navigation Co. were to receive all tolls taken via the Beeston Cut. The Trent Navigation Co. rejected this, at the same time informing the Nottingham Co. the Trent Act did not permit the use of the river as a feeder for the canal.

The Trent Navigation Co. did, however, have a canal of its own in mind which did not get sufficient support at first but finally received its Act of Parliament in 1794. No major works were involved and only two locks were required, one of which was the entrance lock from the river Trent, 14ft 6in (4.408m) wide and 85ft (25.840m) long with a fall of 5ft 2in (1.574m) from the river. The second lock was also an entrance lock into the river which dropped boats back into the river below

BEESTON LOCKS. NOTTS.

Beeston Lock in the early 1900s. The main river lock is to the right; the gates of the second lock
back into the river Trent. Below, Beeston Weir can be seen in front of a row of cottages on the left.
This second lock had flood gates fitted at the river end to stop water flowing back into the canal in
times of flood; the river was only used for shallow draft craft, as it was is shallow in places between
Nottingham and Beeston. (Nottingham County Library Local History Department)

Beeston weir. It was for craft with a shallow draft that were able to ride the flow of
the river and did not need to use the wharves in Nottingham. This lock is on the
right side of the main entrance lock when travelling in the direction of Nottingham
and had a fall into the river of approximately 6–7ft (1.830–2.134m). It was a unique
lock in that it had eight gates, four of which worked in the normal way, the high
water side facing the canal, and four stop gates with the high water side facing the
river. These would be brought into use when the river was in flood to protect the
canal from floodwater. The second lock has now been blocked off and no longer
leads into the river Trent below the weir. The chamber still contains water and is
used for mooring two narrow boats. All gates were removed many years ago; on
the canal side it's possible to see where they had been fixed. On the river side it is
banked up. There is a footbridge over the second lock; the canal can be reached by
crossing the footbridge on the main lock and walking round the front of the lock
house. The lock house is in fine condition with pleasant views looking down the
canal.

The Act, when passed, did in the end allow for the river Trent to be used as a
feeder for supplying water, so as not to use the existing supply of the Nottingham
Canal. This proved to be a very satisfactory arrangement and it is still in use,
and is the main water supply for 5-mile section of canal from Beeston Lock to
Trent Lock where the Nottingham Canal enters the river Trent. The engineer

Above: Boats inside Beeston Lock leaving the river Trent in 2004.

Left: Entrance to the second lock now used for mooring two boats; there are no longer any gates fitted and the river end is sealed off.

was John Bailey, who also did a new survey; he worked under the supervision of William Jessop. Construction was completed in early 1796 and opened to traffic in February the same year. Total cost on completion was £6,141, £1,406 more than the cost in the Nottingham Canal estimate for a Beeston Meadow Branch.

There were no major works involved with just the two locks and five accommodation bridges. Only two of the original five remain, while others have been constructed in recent years to carry new roads.

After a slow start the cut was fairly busy, most of the traffic coming down the river Trent from the Erewash and Derby canals, with long distance traffic from the Trent & Mersey Canal and the Grand Union Canal via the river Soar Navigation.

By the mid-1800s the owner, Trent Navigation Co., which was also the largest user, was suffering from the lack of depth and poor maintenance at the wharves on the Nottingham Canal. Several Acts were passed to allow for improved navigation but little was done. Other attempts were made to improve both the Nottingham Canal and Beeston Cut again in the 1930s but these also fell through. In 1936 the 2½ miles of the Nottingham Canal through Nottingham was leased to the Trent Navigation Co. by the then owners London North Eastern Railway. This gave the control of the 5 miles from the river Trent in Beeston to the river in Nottingham. The remaining 12¼ miles of the Nottingham Canal above Lenton was abandoned one year later. The cut never came under railway control, always being in the hands of the Trent Navigation Co. until it was nationalised in 1948. It is now under the control of British Waterways.

The first 100m of the Beeston Cut runs straight from the lock with the towpath on the left side. The towpath is only a short distance and becomes a road, aptly named 'Canal Side'. There are a number of properties along the road facing the canal as far as the first bridge. The canal here is very busy on both sides with many boats moored. One boat moored along here is the 57ft narrow boat *Iduno*, which was featured in the television programme 'Waterworld'. On the right side over the bank is Beeston Ryelands sports field which for many years had two old railway wagons for changing rooms, a very cold place to change on a winter's day. They were removed a few years ago and replaced by proper changing rooms. The bank on the right is higher than the normal ground because it carries the river Trent flood bank for about a mile very close to the canal side before it turns right across the fields.

At the end of Canal Side, where it meets Meadow Road is the first bridge, a change-over or roving bridge where the towpath changes sides, and it remains like this for the rest of its journey until it meets the Nottingham Canal. Both towpaths meet on the same side at Lenton Chain. Once over the bridge, the towpath is in excellent condition and is perenially busy with walkers. This bridge is in fair condition and still carries some light traffic, mainly to the sports fields on the other side of the canal below the flood bank on land between the canal and the river Trent. This bridge is also an unusual shape; from a distance it appears slightly lop-sided. On examination it seems to have been this way for a long time, but it's doubtful it would have been built that shape in the first place.

From the bridge the excellent towpath is bordered by a concrete wall that supports the flood bank. On the opposite side for approximately 200m there are a number of houses backing onto the waterway from Cornwall Avenue followed by another recreation ground. The canal runs almost straight for over a mile with only a short swing from left to right. Along this section a footbridge passes over on its way down to the river Trent coming down from Beeston, passing between the sewage works and Boots Pharmaceutical Works. Between the sewer works and the last recreation ground lies a piece of very wet ground known as the sludge beds. The towpath passes here just before reaching the canal footbridge.

After the footbridge now comes Boots Pharmaceutical Works (Boots the chemist), which stretches a long way along the side of the cut here. The smell of

Typical Sunday morning on the Beeston Cut in 1977; the lock is in the distance in the centre. Note the first two anglers have their thermos flasks out ready for a warm drink.

perfumes lingers in the air along this stretch, drifting over from the works; also along here are two large water intakes followed further on by two outlets. It would seem they are still taking water from the cut for use in some part of their manufacturing processes. The canal has now reached the aforementioned slight turn from the left to the right before straightening out to pass under the new Thane Road Bridge, one of the entrances into Boots Works. The site of an old canal bridge a short distance before the new bridge can still be found. The bridge was removed some years ago. The canal still narrows here as it did when the bridge was in place. So far the canal water appears reasonably deep and clear, this could be due to the water entering from the river Trent which has been cleaned up greatly in the last few years; the river is now one of the cleanest in the British Isles. Past the flood bank, the high ground on the far side of the river Trent can be seen in the distance.

There is very little on the towpath side now except for a string of electric pylons stretching out across the fields. Once under the bridge it becomes much more pleasant for a short distance with good banks on both sides. The canal now swings left then runs straight again and becomes double width. It remains wide now until the next bridge, Redfield Road Bridge. There are now some small factories opposite the towpath and an industrial estate towpath side behind the high embankment out of site of the canal. When under Redfield Road Bridge the canal starts to narrow and turns right. The high bank remains on the towpath side, behind which there is a ten pin bowling alley, a cinema and a nightclub. This area has been transformed over the last twenty years from what used to be waste ground used as a council tip. On the opposite side on Harrimans Lane and Gibbons Street a number of car scrap yards have been there for many years. The canal is now passing through Dunkirk, a suburb of Nottingham. With all the scrap yards in one area, this is one of the best places in Nottingham for second-hand car spares.

The first bridge on the Beeston Cut at the junction of Meadow Road and Canal Side; as well as being an unusual shape it is also a change-over bridge, the towpath coming over from the right to the left, where it remained for its meeting with the Nottingham Canal towpath at Lenton. This was 1977.

The next point of interest is an original canal bridge, in fine condition, now only used by pedestrians to cross the canal from Gibbons Street to Redfield Way. Access to the towpath is also available here. The canal runs straight from the bridge, passing under a railway bridge that carries the main line into Nottingham from Trent Junction via Attenborough and Beeston. The next bridge is once again a new road bridge, Clifton Boulevard (A614); it is more like a small tunnel than a bridge being about 20–25m in length. Work on the bridge started in August 1956 and it was half completed before the old canal bridge was demolished on Thursday 17 January 1957. Work was completed on the new bridge in May 1957. Leaving this bridge, the last on this short waterway, the towpath continues all the way up to the junction with the Nottingham Canal. On the side away from the towpath there is a small football ground belonging to a school, followed by Dunkirk Fire Station, a branch of Nottingham Fire Service.

Next are some houses with gardens backing onto the waterway there are a number of craft moored at bottom of these gardens. One particular garden has been transformed into a show of all kinds of models and signs to amuse passing boaters and walkers alike. The canal narrows two thirds down this last 75m at the site of where a pair of stop gates was once fitted many years ago. It is still possible to see the location for the gates in the canal wall.

It is now only a few metres from the junction at Lenton Chain where the two waterways meet. There was once a towpath bridge over the entrance to the Beeston Cut carrying the Nottingham Canal towpath.

The Beeston Cut can be very busy with local anglers so care is needed both walking the towpath and travelling by boat. A number of cyclists also use this route into Nottingham, in doing so avoiding the busy roads.

Above: The last original bridge over the Beeston Cut just before its junction with Nottingham Canal at Lenton, in 2004.

Left: New bridge under construction over the Beeston Cut at Lenton to replace the old hump-backed canal bridge, in August 1956. (Peter Stevenson)

Work demolishing the old canal bridge at Lenton, ready for completing the new bridge, which was half complete by January 1957. (Peter Stevenson)

DISTANCE TABLE

Mileage	Description
½	Junction with West Croft Branch
¾	Poplar Arm
1	Brewery Cut
1⅛	Offices of Fellows, Morton & Clayton (Canal Carries)
1¼	Castle Lock No.2
1½	Earl Manvers Canal
2⅛	Leathermill Lock No.3
2¼	Hicklings Lock No.4
2³/₈	Simpsons Lock No.5
2³/₈	Toll Office
2½	Radford Bridge Lock No.6
2½	Radford Wharf (Maintenance Yard & Workshop)
2⅝	Lime Kiln Lock No.7
2¹¹/₁₆	Jackie Mathew's Farm and Wharf
2¾	Black Lock No.8
3	Bottom of First Three No.9
3⅛	Middle of First Three No.10 First Flight of Three
3¼	Top of First Three No.11
3½	No official name, known locally as Woodyard Lane Lock No.12
3¾	Blacksmiths Lock No.13
4	Bottom of Top Three No.14
4¹/₁₆	Middle of Top Three No.15 Second Flight of Three
4⅛	Top of Top Three No.16
4½	Bottom of Woodend Lock No.17
5¼	Top of Woodend Lock No.18
5¼	Wollaton Lock No.19
5¼	Junction with Bilborough Cut
8¼	Trowell Village
9⅞	Junction with Robbinetts Arm
9⅞	Start of Cossall Embankment
10¼	Cossall Village
11½	Awsworth Village
11¾	Junction with Greasley Arm
14¹¹/₁₆	Langley Mill Stop Lock No.20
14¾	Junction with Cromford & Erewash Canals
14¾	Toll Office

Distances are taken from the bottom end of the canal, river Trent end. Some of the distances are correct whilst others are approximate; for instance, it is known that all the locks came within the first 5¼ miles from No.1 at Trent mouth Nottingham to No.19 at Wollaton. I have worked out from this the approximate distance of other locks from local maps and my knowledge of the canal and the area. I believe them to be correct to within a few metres.

LOCK SIZES

Nottingham Canal locks giving sizes, depth, rise and cubic capacity.
Depth is water in lock when at lower level.
Rise is height from lower level to full level.
For total depth when full add the two together.

Lock Name	Size	Depth	Rise	Cubic Capacity
Trent	85ft 4in x 14ft 9in	4ft 8in	8ft 8in	10.908cu. ft
No.1	25.94m x 4.48m	1.42m	2.64m	305.4cu. m
Castle	86ft 1in x 15ft 0in	4ft 6in	4ft 6in	5.838cu. ft
No.2	26.17m x 4.56m	1.37m	1.37m	163.46cu. m
Leathermill	85ft 0in x 14ft 10in	4ft 10in	6ft 4in	8.032cu. ft
No.3	25.84m x 4.51m	1.47m	1.93m	224.89cu. m
Hicklings	85ft 9in x 14ft 9in	4ft 6in	6ft 8in	8.431cu. ft
No.4	26.07m x 4.48m	1.37m	2.06m	236.06cu. m
Simpsons	85ft 9in x 15ft 0in	6ft 4in	7ft 6in	9.646cu. ft
No.5	26.07m x 4.56m	1.93m	2.28m	270.08cu. m
Radford Bridge	86ft 3in x 14ft 9in	5ft 2in	8ft 9in	11.131cu. ft
No.6	26.22m x 4.48m	1.57m	2.66m	311.66cu. m
Limekiln	85ft 8in x 14ft 9in	4ft 7in	6ft 9in	8.529cu. ft
No.7	26.04m x 4.48m	1.40m	2.06m	238.81cu. m
Black	85ft 9in x 14ft9in	4ft 6in	7ft 2in	9.054cu. ft
No.8	26.07m x 4.48m	1.37m	2.18m	253.51cu. m
Bottom of 1st Three No.9	85ft 9in x 15ft 0in 26.07m x 4.56m	4ft 6in 1.37m	6ft 7in 2.01m	8.468cu. ft 237.10cu. m
Middle of 1st Three No.10	87ft 0in x 15ft 0in 26.45m x 4.56m	5ft 2in 1.57m	6ft 4in 1.93m	8.265cu. ft 231.42cu. m
Top of 1st Three No.11	85ft 9in x 15ft 0in 26.09m x 4.56m	4ft 9in 1.45m	8ft 3in 2.51m	10.611cu. ft 297.28cu. m
Woodyard Lane No.12	86ft 3in x 14ft 6in 26.22m x 4.41m	4ft 8in 1.42m	6ft 10in 2.08m	8.546cu. ft 239.28cu. m
Blacksmiths No.13	85ft 0in x 14ft 6in 25.840m x 4.41m	4ft 6in 1.37m	7ft 6in 2.29m	9 244cu. ft 258.83cu. m
Bottom of Top Three No.14	86ft 0in x 14ft 7in 26.14m x 4.43m	4ft 6in 1.37m	6ft 7in 2.00m	8.256cu. ft 231.16cu. m
Middle of Top	86ft 0in x 14ft 7in	4ft 6in	7ft 1in	8.883cu. ft

Three No.15	26.14m x 4.43m	1.37m	2.16m	248.72cu. m
Bottom of Top	86ft 0in x 14ft 9in	4ft 11in	7ft 2in	9.090cu. ft
Three No.16	26.14m x 4.48m	1.50m	2.18m	254.52cu. m
Bottom Wood	85ft 3in x 14ft 9in	4ft 7in	5ft 4in	6.706cu. ft
End No.17	25 91m x 4.48m	1.40m	1.62m	187.76cu. m
Top Woodend	87ft 0in x 14ft 6in	4ft 2in	8ft 3in	10.407cu. ft
No.18	26.45m x 4.41m	1.27m	2.51m	291.39cu. m
Wollaton	86ft 4in x 14ft 6in	5ft 0in	6ft 10in	8.554cu. ft
No.19	26.24m x 4.41m	1.600m	2.08m	239.51cu. m
Langley Mill	89ft 0in x 15ft 0in	5ft 3in	Nil	Nil
Stop Lock No.20	27.05m x 4.56m	4.56m	Nil	Nil

The average discharge of water per lock from No.1 to No.19 was 8.874cu. ft (221.85cu. m) 55,462 gallons (252.13l).

BRIDGES

List of bridges on the canal at the time of construction, type and material used, height and span over canal given for first eighteen bridges only. From Bridge No.20 most were wooden swing bridges probably built for the use of local farmers, with only fixed bridges built where small roads crossed the canal. So much destruction has taken place since the canal was abandoned, mostly through open-cast coal mining, that no information could be found for bridge nos 29 to 32, with local maps being unclear.

Bridges	Type	Height	Span
No.1	Stone Arch Bridge	10ft 8in	21ft 9in
Meadow Lane	3.311m	6.612m	
No.2	Stone Arch Bridge	14ft 3in	30ft 2 ½in
Change Over	3.835m	9.196in	
No.3	Wrought-iron girder	8ft 6in	47ft 1in
Footbridge	2.616m	14.288m	
No.4	Wooden Bridge	9ft 6in	21ft 7in
Trent Street	2.895m	6.536m	
No.5	Wooden Bridge	8ft 7in	20ft 11in
Claytons	2.641m	6.360m	
No.6	Brick Arch Bridge	9ft 5in	21ft 6in
Gregory Street	2.870m	6.536m	
No.7	Brick Arch Bridge	11ft 0in	21ft 11in
Abbey Road	3.844m	6.685m	
No.8	Iron Girder & Wood	8ft 7in	22ft 5in
Leengate Footbridge	2.641m	6.840m	
No.9	Brick Arch Bridge	9ft 8in	24ft 5in
Derby Road	2.946m	7.445m	
No.10	Brick Arch Bridge	9ft 10in	22ft 2in
Radford Bridge Road	2.997m	6.764m	
No.11	Brick with Wooden Top	9ft 3in	21ft 5in
Woodyard Lane	2.819m	6.536m	
No.12	Brick Arch Bridge	9ft 9in	21ft 10in
Coach Road	2.971m	6.612m	
No.13	Brick Arch Bridge	9ft 2in	22ft 5in
Wollaton	2.794m	6.840m	
No.14	Stone Arch Bridge	10ft 5in	21ft 3in
Stackyard	3.175m	6.460m	
No.15	Stone Arch Bridge	11ft 1in	27ft 0in

Bramcote Moo	3.378m	8.208m	
No.16	Stone Arch Bridge	9ft 2in	22ft 1in
Coventry Lane	2.794m	6.690m	
No.17	Stone Arch Bridge	not known	not known
Potters Bridge			
No.18	Stone Arch Bridge	not known	not known
Swansea Bridge			
No.19	Stone Arch Bridge	not known	not known
Trowell Bridge			
No.20	Swing Bridge	Towpath Level	not given
Marriots Bridge			
No.21	Swing Bridge	Towpath Level	not given
No Name			
No.22	Swing Bridge	Towpath Level	not given
Robbinetts			
No.23	Swing Bridge	Towpath Level	not given
No Name			
No.24	Swing Bridge	Towpath Level	not given
Mill Lane			
No.25	Swing Bridge	Towpath Level	not given
No Name			
No.26	Brick Arch	not known	not known
Newtons Lane			
No.27	Brick Arch	not known	not known
Park Hill			
No.28	Brick Arch	not known	not known
No name			
No.29	not known	not known	not known
Not known			
No.30	not known	not known	not known
Not known			
No.31	not known	not known	not known
Not known			
No.32	not known	not known	not known
Not known			
No.33	Swing Bridge	Towpath Level	not given
No name			
No.34	Brick Arch	not known	not known
Tinsley Road			
No.35	Brick with wooden top	not known	not known
Anchor Bridge			
No.36	Swing Bridge	Towpath Level	not given
Langley Mill			

General Bibliography

Books

Nottingham Canal Minute Books 1790 to 1856
Canals of the East Midlands, Charles Hadfield (1966 David & Charles)
Bradshaw Canals & Navigable Rivers, H.R. De-Salis (reprinted David & Charles 1969)
Nottingham Canal Act

Magazines and Newspapers

Nottingham Weekly Post Nos 298, 316 and 322
Beeston Gazette & Echo No.4067, 23 December 1976
Nottingham Canal News-sheet, September 1973
Railway & Historical Society, East Midlands Group leaflet (notes for tour cruise from Meadow Lane to Trent Lock) 5 May 1974
Lenton Times issue No.2. (Lenton Local History Society)
Nottingham Canal News-Sheet (Sheila M Cooke)
Nottingham Evening Post (Publishers T. Bailey Forman Ltd)

Other Sources

Records of the Borough of Nottingham
British Waterways
Nottingham County Library Local History Department
British Transport Commission Historical Records

Acknowledgments

T. Bailey Forman, publishers of *Nottingham Evening Post & Weekly Post*
Kirk publications for *Beeston Gazette & Echo*
Nottingham Historical Film Unit for Canal Company Seal
Mr Peter Stevenson (Author of *Nutbrook Canal*) for help and information on the Cossall Aqueduct
Broxtowe Borough Council for help given, especially Mr Steve Fisher
Nottingham Records Office, principal archivist and staff

Photographs

Broxtowe Borough Council
Nottingham County Library Local History Department
Mr Peter Stevenson
Mr R. Berry
Unless otherwise stated, all photographs are from my own collection

Documents

Nottingham County Library Local History Department
Nottingham Historical Film Unit
Sketch map & drawing by my son Kevin
Broxtowe Borough Council

I would very much like to thank all the above for their help and advice, which was freely given in the preparation of this book

INDEX

If you are interested in purchasing other books published by Tempus,
or in case you have difficulty finding any Tempus books in your local bookshop,
you can also place orders directly through our website

www.tempus-publishing.com